IMMIGRATION

IMMIGRATION

BY LYDIA ANDERSON

FRANKLIN WATTS
New York/London/Toronto/Sydney/1981
AN IMPACT BOOK

FOR JIMMY
and for our good friends who
have come to this country
from other lands and so
enriched our lives

Photographs courtesy of:
The Museum of the City of New York/Jacob Riis: frontispiece
Culver Pictures, Inc.: pp. 3 and 16
The Bettmann Archive, Inc.: p. 23
New York Public Library Picture Collection: pp. 30 and 74
United Press International, Inc.: pp. 43, 49, and 56

Library of Congress Cataloging in Publication Data

Anderson, Lydia.
    Immigration.

    "An Impact book."
    Bibliography: p.
    Includes index.
    Summary: Traces the history of immigration
into the United States from the seventeenth century
to the present and discusses the varying policies
governing entry into this country with emphasis on
such problems as quotas, illegal aliens, and refugees.
    1. United States—Emigration and immigration—
History—Juvenile literature. [1. United States—
Emigration and immigration—History] I. Title.

JV6450.A63	325.73	81–3432
ISBN 0–531–04335–5		AACR2

CONTENTS

IMMIGRATION

---

*Remember, remember always, that all of us . . .
are descended from immigrants and revolutionists.*

FRANKLIN D. ROOSEVELT

Here is not merely a nation,
but a teeming nation of nations.
Walt Whitman

INTRODUCTION

America is a nation of immigrants. Twenty of every hundred of us are either foreign-born or children of foreign-born parents. The rest of us are descended from immigrants of earlier generations.

Since 1607, when the English founded the colony of Jamestown, Virginia, nearly 50 million people of all races, religions, cultures, customs, and traditions have left their homelands to come to this country in search of political freedom, religious tolerance, and economic opportunity.

The first wave of immigrants settled our Atlantic coast in the seventeenth century. Those who followed in the eighteenth century extended our frontiers to the Allegheny Mountains. In the nineteenth century, immigrants helped to open the West, stimulate the growth of our cities, and foster the development of our burgeoning industries.

In the hundred years between 1820, when immigration records were first kept, and 1920, nearly two-thirds of all the people who emigrated from any country in the world came to the United States. This mass migration was unique in history.

Uprooted from their native lands, the immigrants faced the hardship of a long and difficult journey. Leaving the security of their small home towns and villages, they faced the loneliness of our big cities or of our vast plains and prairies. They were forced to adjust to a new environment in a strange country different in many ways from their own. Many of them had to learn a new language. In order to earn a living, they often had to master a new trade or different type of job: farmers became construction workers; teachers became machine operators; peddlers ran pushcarts or entered the garment and jewelry trades.

And each new wave of immigrants, in turn, had to struggle for the acceptance of earlier immigrants who often found their accents, dress, religion, and even appearance, offensive.

In spite of the sufferings, the struggles, and the confrontations, immigrants built America and made it the diversified nation it is today.

An immigrant is a person other than a citizen who is allowed to settle permanently in the United States. For the first hundred years after independence, immigrants were welcomed with few reservations. But, as the frontier closed, the cities became crowded, competition for jobs increased, and resentment against open immigration grew.

The first restrictive legislation was passed in 1882, barring Chinese. Subsequent measures introduced a literacy test as a requirement for immigration, quotas based on national origins, and, at one time, exclusion based solely on race.

Mass migration peaked between 1905 and 1914 when an average of a million immigrants a year came to the United States. Two world wars, a devastating depression in the 1930s, and restrictive legislation limited the numbers for the next half

**The symbol of a new life:
the Statue of Liberty seen
from an incoming ship.**

century. By the end of the 1970s, however, poverty and unrest around the world swelled the number of legal immigrants,
many of them refugees, to over half a million a year. In addition, untold numbers entered illegally. Immigration at the end
of the century began to match that at the start.

Millions of people apply for immigration to the United
States every year. As long as conditions are better *here* than
they are *there,* they will continue to do so.

Discriminatory quotas and racist exclusion are now largely
gone. But, we are still seeking answers to the questions which
have plagued us for the past one hundred years:

How many immigrants should we admit?

*From which countries, or regions, or
hemispheres should they come?*

*What conditions should determine
their eligibility for admission?*

Our country was founded as a haven for the oppressed and
downtrodden of the world. Can we continue to support large-
scale immigration without compromising our own standard
of living? Today, more than ever before, we Americans face a
conflict between the humanitarian precepts of the past and our
own self-interest in the future.

What, then, is this new man,
the American? They are a mixture
of English, Scotch, Irish, French,
Dutch, Germans, and Swedes. From
this promiscuous breed, that race,
now called Americans, have arisen.
                              J. Hector St. John
                              de Crevecoeur

FOUNDING A NEW NATION

The story of immigration is the story of America. Even the people we call Native Americans were originally migrants from another continent. Sometime between 30,000 and 13,000 B.C., when the last Ice Age lowered the waters of the Pacific Ocean, they crossed the Bering Straits from Asia and, seeking hunting and fishing grounds and a warmer climate, progressed slowly across North America and southward into Mexico and Central and South America. There were probably fewer than a million of them in the lands we now know as the United States when the first Europeans came to our country, mistakenly named them Indians, and learned from them the cultivation of corn, tobacco, and potatoes.

A few adventurous Norsemen may have reached our shores as early as the eleventh century, but the Spanish, seeking gold, silver, and cheap and plentiful labor, were the first Europeans to arrive in number. They followed the American Indians by some 115 centuries. Ponce de León sailed into Florida in

1513. Pánfilo de Narváez and Hernando de Soto explored the territories along the Gulf of Mexico between 1528 and 1542. Francisco Vásquez de Coronado, in search of the fabled riches of the "Seven Cities of Cíbola," explored the American Southwest from Texas to California.

These expeditions found little to encourage them to stay. Precious metals were few, and the Indian population was too scarce or uncooperative to exploit. In 1565, however, the Spanish established a fort and mission at Saint Augustine, Florida, making it our oldest city. By 1762, at its peak, Spanish territory stretched from Florida to California and, west of the Mississippi, as far north as the Canadian border.

Although few Spanish explorers, missionaries, or conquistadors settled here permanently, Spanish culture had a lasting influence on our architecture, music, art, and dance. It also contributed many words to our language, established the form of the great ranches of the West, and gave eight states their Spanish names: Arizona, California, Colorado, Florida, Montana, New Mexico, Nevada, and Texas.

In the twentieth century, a new wave of Hispanics, descendants of the conquistadors, would affect the ethnic character of the country even more.

COLONIAL SETTLERS

The first English colony was established at Jamestown, Virginia, in 1607, to "fetch treasure" and enjoy the benefits of a "religious and happy government." The English, unlike the Spanish, came to this country to stay and were the first Europeans to settle here in large numbers. They came to make new homes in an atmosphere of religious and political freedom and to escape oppressive economic conditions in the British Isles. They also came to extend the British Empire overseas and to provide it with a source of raw materials and a market for manufactured goods.

British Pilgrims founded Plymouth, Massachusetts, in 1620 to "advance the gospel . . . in those remote parts of the world"; British Puritans, seeking religious freedom, founded Massachusetts Bay Colony in 1630; British Catholics settled in Maryland in 1634; British Quakers, led by William Penn, founded Pennsylvania in 1681, as a "holy experiment" in brotherhood. Georgia was founded by James Oglethorpe in 1733 as an asylum for poor British debtors. British courtiers, seeking their fortunes, settled in the Carolinas in 1670.

An Act of the British Parliament in 1717 made transportation to the colonies proper punishment for certain crimes. Some 30,000 offenders were shipped from English jails, mostly to Virginia and Maryland, making the practice of "dumping" one's undesirables an old one.

Explorers, traders, adventurers, indentured servants, aristocrats and paupers, merchants, missionaries, and farmers, the British shaped the new nation. They gave us our laws, our system of government, our tradition of religious tolerance, and our language.

Colonial governments encouraged immigration by supplying transportation, food, land, and equipment to immigrants. Exemption from military duty, universal male suffrage, and a humane penal code also attracted immigrants.

The colonial population grew to 52,000 in 1650; 275,000 in 1700; and over a million by 1750. When the first census was taken in 1790, it counted 3,227,000 people, nearly 80 percent of them of British origin, including numbers of Scotch-Irish and Welsh.

Nearly everyone else, including the few Spanish who remained, was from western Europe, as well. The Dutch settled New Amsterdam in 1624. They brought us their tulips, sleds, and Santa Claus; formed the great farming estates of the Hudson River Valley; bought Manhattan Island from the Indians for twenty-four dollars and named Breuckelen and the Bronck.

Swedes set up trading posts in Delaware in 1638. They gave us that sturdy dwelling of the frontier, the log cabin.

The French explored the Mississippi Valley extensively, profited from fur trading, and founded New Orleans in 1718. French influence is still discernible in that city's food and language, in the French Quarter and the ambience of Creole life. A small group of French Huguenots, Protestants fleeing religious persecution in France, settled in South Carolina in 1685. French Acadians fled from Nova Scotia to Louisiana in 1755 after the English captured the territory and expelled them under suspicion of disloyalty.

Germans accounted for 8.7 percent of the colonial population. Thirteen German families settled in Philadelphia between 1660 and 1685. Germany has since sent 7 million immigrants to our shores, more than any other country. "America, you have it better than our old continent," wrote their poet Goethe.

The first Jewish immigrants came to America in 1654, twenty-three refugees fleeing persecution by the Portuguese in Brazil. At the time of the American Revolution, there were about 2,000 of them in the colonies, where they enjoyed more religious freedom than had been granted them elsewhere.

The first black slaves arrived at the plantations of Virginia in 1619. They were the first immigrants, after the English, to come as permanent settlers, albeit against their wills. About 350,000 Africans were brought into the country over the next 200 years. Under what the South called its "peculiar institution," they supplied labor for sugar, tobacco, and cotton plantations: hard work under broiling sun in open fields which American Indians could not survive. Often taken as captives by warring African tribes, they were sold to slave traders in exchange for cloth, beads, rum, and guns, and shipped under brutal conditions to the "New World." Theirs was a forced migration in which they largely lost their culture and identity as Africans. We called them "Negroes." Their labor helped the American economy grow. Today, their descendants form 11.7 percent of our population.

Together, these people built a new nation, and they started what was to become, in the next century, the greatest movement of people in the history of the world.

POST-REVOLUTIONARY PERIOD
Immigration was encouraged after the Revolutionary War. British restriction of immigration to the colonies was one of the "repeated injuries and usurpations" charged against

George III in the Declaration of Independence. George Washington declared in 1783:

The bosom of America is open to receive not only the opulent and respectable stranger, but the oppressed and persecuted of all nations and religions . . .

Many hands were needed to clear, develop, and settle the land, to protect the colonists and their property from the threat of Indian attack, and to take the land from the Indians as the westward movement progressed. There was space enough for people of different cultures to preserve their own customs and traditions without offending others. The country was huge, the frontiers broad, and individual opportunity seemingly endless.

For thirty-six years after the Revolution, immigration was slight: only about 7,000 people a year came to the United States. Wars in Europe closed the sea routes and disrupted communications between the continents.

Then, in the sixty years between 1820 and 1880, the number of immigrants swelled to 10 million.

So at last I was going to America!
Really, really going, at last!
The boundaries burst. The arch of
heaven soared. A million suns shone
out for every star. The winds
rushed in from outer space, roaring
in my ears, "America! America!"
                                    Mary Antin

THE FIRST WAVE: 1820-1880

From 8,000 in 1820; to 23,000 in 1830; to 84,000 in 1840; over 100,000 immigrants arrived in 1845 and 459,000 in 1873!

With Europe at peace after 1815, commerce was resumed and expanded around the world, providing ships for transport. Regular service to New York by sailing packet began in 1818. Liverpool, England, Le Havre, France, and Bremen, Germany, were major points of embarkation. Poverty and crime abounded in these crowded port cities. The ocean voyages sometimes took as long as three months, often in treacherous weather. Food and water often gave out. Quarters in steerage, below deck, were cramped and airless. Sanitary facilities were poor or lacking altogether. Diseases such as cholera, yellow fever, and smallpox were common. About one person in ten died enroute to America. A ship's passenger list in the year 1849 showed 475 sick, 658 dead, and 76 born in passage. A ratio of 60 percent illness was not unusual.

What led 10 million people to endure these hardships?

During the nineteenth century, the population of Europe increased enormously. Poor harvests were common. Peasants were no longer able to support themselves and their families on their land. They fled to the cities, which could not satisfy the demand for jobs. The Industrial Revolution displaced many skilled craftsmen who were not content to take factory jobs. The European social structure was rigid. There was little mobility between social classes. The peasants had little to look forward to but an endless struggle to feed and clothe themselves.

The United States, on the other hand, was enjoying an expanding economy and jobs were available at good wages. Peasants, farmers, miners, artisans . . . all were needed and welcome. The gold the Spanish had sought was discovered in 1848. Rich coal and iron deposits were to be mined; cities to be built; mills to be manned. Free land was offered to settlers who would develop it and help open the route west for the railroads. Political freedom and religious tolerance beckoned. So did ship and railroad agents seeking passengers, employers' representatives seeking labor, and landowners seeking tenants. They had no trouble finding takers. The price of the trip was right, too. It was sometimes as low as ten dollars a head.

Castle Garden, at the tip of Manhattan Island, opened in 1855 to process the mass of immigrants entering New York City. By 1892, it was no longer adequate and a larger facility opened at Ellis Island where it operated as an immigration center until 1932. After 1924, immigrants were inspected in their countries of origin. Ellis Island is now an immigration museum.

Many Swedes left home after crop failures in the 1860s. French, Norwegians, English, and Dutch continued to emigrate, too. But the bulk of the "old immigration," as this first wave would later be called, came from Germany and Ireland.

FROM GERMANY

Germans arrived in large numbers between 1840 and 1850 fleeing political unrest, crop failures, mortgage foreclosures, and poor trade prospects. The "48ers" were middle-class liberals and intellectuals, taking flight from reactionary governments at home.

Americans did not approve of the Germans' beer halls or their Sunday revelry but eventually the Germans, or "Dutch" (for *Deutsch*), as they were called, came to be thought of as model citizens. Their neat farms and tidy homes were admired. They brought with them their love of classical music, their proficiency in printing and papermaking, their enthusiasm for physical culture, education, and social and political planning. They gave us our covered wagons, our kindergartens and gymnasiums, frankfurters, cole slaw and dill pickles, as well as Pabst, Schlitz, Miller, and Budweiser beers. John F. Kennedy wrote that we owed to the Germans "the mellowing of the austere Puritan imprint on our daily lives."

FROM IRELAND

The Irish, wasted by the potato famine of 1845–47 and the economic and religious restrictions imposed by England, fled from misery and starvation to our shores. By 1860, 2 million of them had come; by 1920, over 4 million. Largely unskilled and uneducated, and poorer than the Germans, they were seldom able to move beyond the big cities of the Northeast, where they settled in "shanty towns" and took the hardest and most menial jobs as construction workers, ditchdiggers, longshoremen, canal and railroad builders, textile mill workers, coal miners, washerwomen, and domestic servants.

They established themselves early in city politics, often to the consternation of others. "Our Celtic friends are good at voting, they vote early and sometimes often, and as a general thing can be relied upon for the whole Democratic ticket," reported one Boston newspaper. They also helped build our police forces.

The Irish tended to be heavy drinkers and their rowdyism was deplored. But they brought us their lighthearted lilting music and their jigs and reels and clogs, and their Irish humor helped establish our theater. A popular ditty of 1865 made fun of the discrimination the Irish worker faced:

I'm a decent boy just landed
From the town of Ballyfad
I want a situation yes
And I want it very bad

I've seen employment advertised
Just the thing says I
But the dirty rascal ended with
"No Irish need apply"

In addition to providing economic benefits, America offered asylum to political émigrés of many liberal movements which rose and fell in Germany, Hungary, Ireland, Italy, and Poland during the nineteenth century.

America continued to be a land of refuge as well as a land of opportunity.

Give me your tired, your poor,
Your huddled masses yearning to breathe
  free,
The wretched refuse of your teeming
  shore,
Send these, the homeless, tempest-tossed,
  to me:
I lift my lamp beside the golden door.
                                    Emma Lazarus

THE FLOOD TIDE: 1880-1920

On July 4, 1884, the "Statue of Liberty Enlightening the World" was officially accepted by the American people as a gift from France. For nearly a hundred years thereafter, her majestic figure welcomed the "huddled masses" of the world.

Between 1880 and 1920, immigration hit all-time highs. Over 23.5 million aliens entered the United States. Ten million came in the years between 1905 and 1914 alone, with over a million coming in each of six years: 1905, 1906, 1907, 1910, 1913, and 1914.

Travel conditions improved. At mid-century, sailing ships transported 96 percent of the immigrants. By the end of the century, steamships provided 96 percent of the transportation and laws were passed to improve conditions of travel, including the provision of food and cooking stoves for steerage passengers.

Improved communications spread the word about opportunity in the United States. Families who had entered in the first wave wrote home, sent money for passage, and urged friends and relatives to follow them. Employers and steamship companies added their encouragement.

And so they came in droves.

But they came from different sources.

Up to 1882, 95 percent of the immigrants came from the British Isles, Germany, France, Belgium, and Scandinavia, the countries of northern and western Europe. In the decade that closed the period, 1911–20, 77 percent came from southern and eastern Europe: 60 percent from Italy, Russia, and Austria-Hungary and many others from Bulgaria, Greece, Poland, Portugal, Rumania, Spain, and Turkey. Between 1881 and 1920, we received 4 million Italians and 4 million Austro-Hungarians, most of whom were Catholics, and 3 million Russians, almost all Jews fleeing government-organized persecution or *pogroms* at home.

In northern and western Europe, the birthrate was declining. Famine had been relieved in Ireland and employment was high in Germany and England. Religious and political tolerance grew.

In southern and eastern Europe, however, unemployment, overpopulation, and high birthrates still prevailed. Religious and political oppression continued and social conditions remained poor. The Industrial Revolution had not progressed far enough to offer job opportunities to surplus workers.

Public sentiment reacted to the masses of immigrants and to the shift in sources of origin. The newcomers were dubbed the "new immigration." They looked different from the old. They were darker complexioned. They spoke different languages. They were almost all Catholics or Jews. They were no longer farmers who came to open the West but unskilled laborers who came to work in factories at lower wages and working standards than American workers. Crowded together in city slums and tenements, they were not as easily assimilated as the "old" immigration. They maintained their own language and traditions longer. Their increasing influence in politics and government was resented.

In 1916, Madison Grant's book, *The Passing of the Great*

Race, called for barring these "inferior breeds" in favor of superior Anglo-Saxon and Teutonic peoples. Henry Ford instigated a program of "Americanization" for his workers which sought to impress on them "that their former racial, national, and linguistic differences are to be forgotten." The "melting pot" theory proposed that the most desirable aliens were those who were most quickly and unobtrusively absorbed. The sooner they adopted our clothes and customs and, above all, *learned English,* the better.

Prejudice was not new to America, but with the mass migrations of the early 1900s, it became a major influence on immigration policy.

Immigrants await processing in "the pens" at Ellis Island.

Remember that when you say
"I will have none of this exile and this
stranger
For his face is not like my face and his
speech is strange,"
You have denied America with that word.
                              Stephen Vincent Benet

NATIVISM

Benjamin Franklin wrote testily of the Germans in Philadelphia in the 1750s:

> *Those who have come hither are generally the most stupid of their nation. Not being used to liberty they know not how to make modest use of it. And as Holbein says of the Hottentots, they are not esteemed men until they have shown their manhood by beating their mothers . . .*

The rejection of alien persons and cultures and the favoring of previously established residents in a country is called Nativism. This prejudice, first directed toward the Germans, was later shifted to the Irish, largely because of their Catholicism.

Many of the original settlers had fled from friction between Protestants and Catholics in the Old World and feared renewed conflict if the Catholic Church became established here. Many considered the authority of a Pope even less desirable than that of a King. They also questioned whether

Catholics, owing their first loyalty to the Church, would be free and independent enough to make good citizens. Many felt that separate parochial schools threatened the public school system.

Anti-Catholic riots occurred in New York, Philadelphia, and Boston as early as the 1830s. Convents were burned and Catholic schools stoned.

As the rate of immigration increased, a number of anti-Catholic, anti-foreign organizations sprang into being. The Native American party was founded in 1835 to combat the influence of the Irish in politics. Big city politics were often corrupt and the Irish were blamed. An American Republican party, formed in 1843, opposed public office-holding by the foreign-born. A secret society called the Order of the Star Spangled Banner was founded in 1849. Its members were called Know Nothings, a response they were supposed to give when questioned about their program. They favored a twenty-five years' residency requirement for naturalization and restriction of the rights of aliens to vote and hold office.

Periods of depression, including financial panics in 1837 and 1870, led to movements to restrict immigration. Employers often exploited new workers and paid them poorly. As a result, American workers held the immigrants responsible for lowered wage rates and depressed labor standards. They also charged that immigration was destroying the apprentice system.

As cities became crowded, slums proliferated and crime spread. Taxes rose and the cost of public welfare mounted. Nativists blamed many of the country's economic ills on the new mass of immigrants.

RACISM

As the sources of immigration shifted to southern and eastern Europe, a more strident voice was heard. The newcomers were claimed to be "biologically inferior." Nativists compared the "historically free, energetic, progressive, hardworking people" of northern and western Europe (including the Germans and Irish) to "Slav, Latin, and Asiatic races, historically downtrodden, atavistic and stagnant" who lacked experience in representative government.

Inventor Samuel F. B. Morse referred to the new immigrants as "priest-controlled machines" and railed against "foreign turbulence imported by shiploads."

The President of the Massachusetts Institute of Technology, writing in 1870, called the new immigrants "beaten men from beaten races . . . the worst failures in the struggle for existence." Their native countries were accused of exporting the "dregs of civilization" to our shores.

The American Protective Association of the 1890s called for closing the "floodgates" of immigration and bitterly opposed the entry of Slavs, Sicilians, and other immigrants from southern and eastern Europe, whom they denigrated as "the $9.60 slime." The Immigration Restriction League, formed after the depression of 1893 by a group of Harvard graduates, also emphasized differences between "old" and "new." The Ku Klux Klan—anti-Catholic, anti-Jew, anti-black, and anti-foreign—was active in the anti-immigration campaign.

Still, our nation had been founded on belief in religious tolerance and the tradition of freedom and opportunity for all. Service in the Civil War helped assimilate many immigrants into United States society. Abraham Lincoln inspired a plank of the Republican Party platform of 1864 stating: "foreign immigration, which in the past, has added so much to the wealth, development of resources, and increase of power to the nation—the asylum of the oppressed of all nations—shall be fostered and encouraged by a liberal and just policy."

For a long time, these principles, and our economic needs as a developing nation, took precedence over anti-Catholic and anti-foreign fears.

In times of shrinking expectations,
. . . everyone feels a victim and
pushes away outsiders to defend
his own corner.

Oscar Handlin

THE BEGINNINGS OF RESTRICTION

There was little demand to restrict immigration for over a hundred years after the country's founding. The Alien and Sedition Acts of 1798 gave the President broad powers to deport aliens and raised the residence requirement for citizenship to fourteen years. Enacted as a political measure in an attempt by the Federalists to prevent Thomas Jefferson and his followers from gaining power, most of these laws were repealed after the Republican victory of 1800.

Some states passed laws to protect themselves from receiving immigrants who might become public charges. In 1807, the federal government prohibited importing slaves. Our naturalization laws, which allowed immigrants to become citizens after five years, were the most liberal in the world.

From the start, however, there were expressions of caution. George Washington noted that we would welcome immigrants to participate in our rights and privileges "if by decency and propriety of conduct they appear to merit the enjoyment."

Thomas Jefferson questioned the advisability of allowing monarchists to enter freely. John Quincy Adams stated that immigrants who became citizens would enjoy full rights but warned them not to expect "favors."

For the first hundred years, the only restrictions on immigration were disruptions caused by wars and politics in Europe. Legislation to improve transatlantic travel encouraged immigration. An immigration office was established in the State Department in 1864. It was later transferred to the Treasury and, in 1903, to the Department of Labor.

After the Civil War, we needed immigrant labor to help lay railroads and dig canals, build cities, mine coal and iron, operate textile and steel mills, and run factories. Rich people wanted servants.

National regulation began in 1875 when Congress prohibited the immigration of prostitutes and convicts. The first general immigration statute, passed in 1882, put a head tax of fifty cents on all immigrants and barred undesirables such as idiots, lunatics, and persons apt to become public charges.

In 1882, Congress also enacted our first racist immigration law, the Chinese Exclusion Act. Between 1850 and 1882, some 200,000 Chinese workers had come to our west coast, fleeing famine, flood, overpopulation, and economic deprivation in Canton. They called themselves "Gum Shan Hok," "Guests of the Golden Mountain." Used to hardship and poor living conditions, they were willing to work long hours at hard labor in gold-mining camps and on railroad work gangs. With the completion of the transcontinental railroad in 1869 and a depression in the 1870s, American workers called for banning further entry of "coolie" labor. "They were so many, so thrifty, so uncomplaining, so glad to work at any price, and above all so alien—so strange—so 'heathenish,'" wrote a contemporary American writer.

Violent racist riots drove the Chinese out of manufacturing and mining and into small businesses like laundries. Many of them entered domestic service, where they were not considered to be in competition with native workers.

In 1881, the Workingmen's Party of California, led by

**American reaction against
foreign laborers was harsh.**

Dennis Kearney (an Irish immigrant), helped promote enactment of legislation in California which prohibited hiring Chinese. This paved the way for the federal legislation of 1882 suspending the entry of Chinese laborers for ten years and barring foreign-born Chinese from citizenship. "The Chinese are inferior to any race God ever made," proclaimed a California legislative report. "[They] have no souls to save, and if they have, they are not worth saving."

The Exclusion Act was renewed for ten years in 1892 and in 1902. In 1904, Chinese immigration was indefinitely suspended, not to be resumed until 1943. Many Chinese returned to their homelands. It should be noted that the United States was not alone in restrictionist sentiment at this time. Australia, in 1901, enacted a language test which effectively excluded Asians and Africans.

Japanese workers who came to America to take the place of the Chinese met with similar prejudice and discrimination. In 1905, San Francisco's political bosses ordered segregation of Japanese school children, prompting President Theodore Roosevelt to denounce "the infernal fools in California and especially San Francisco [who] insult the Japanese recklessly."

Businessmen and civic leaders joined with organized labor in forming the Japanese and Korean Exclusion League. To avoid an international crisis, Japan and the United States signed the so-called Gentlemen's Agreement of 1907–1908 in which the Japanese government agreed to deny passports to Japanese workers traveling directly from Japan to the United States. The United States, in return, gave assurances that American law would not discriminate against Japanese aliens already here.

In 1913, however, California barred Japanese from buying land and declared them "aliens ineligible for citizenship." Mixed marriages between Americans and orientals were discouraged. Orientals (like blacks), distinguishable by their physical characteristics, were often subject to the most extreme forms of prejudice. Nativists dubbed orientals the "yellow peril." America was no longer "Dai On Jin," "The Great Friendly People."

The antagonism between Japan and the United States which developed at this time eventually culminated in World War II. During that war, over 100,000 Japanese were interned as "enemy aliens" at concentration camps in the interior of the United States. About two-thirds of them were American-born citizens. None of them were given a chance to prove their loyalty. Americans of Italian and German extraction were allowed to remain free.

In 1890, the Census Bureau declared the frontier closed. This meant the end of the unlimited horizons and seemingly endless potential of the West. As immigrants continued to arrive and the population to grow, they were accused of draining the country's resources and of requiring public funds or private charity to survive.

Between 1882 and 1907, Congress passed laws which barred idiots, lunatics, convicts, persons likely to become public charges, people with "loathsome or dangerous diseases" such as tuberculosis and epilepsy, persons convicted of criminal offenses involving moral turpitude, paupers, polygamists, professional beggars, anarchists and other political radicals, the insane, the feebleminded, persons with mental or physical defects which might prevent them from earning a living, and children under sixteen unaccompanied by their parents.

These exclusions, characterized by one authority as "an accumulation of prejudices," were designed to control the quality and character of the immigrants and to define those considered unfit. (We wanted them to be healthy and to be able to work for a living.) For nearly one hundred fifty years, there was no attempt to limit the *number* who might come.

The United States is our land. If it
was not the land of our fathers, at
least it may be, and should be, the land
of our children. We intend to maintain
it so. The day of unalloyed welcome to all
peoples, the day of indiscriminate accept-
ance of all races, has definitely ended.

Representative Albert Johnson

(1924)

SETTING LIMITS

Disillusion following World War I created a climate of isolationism. The Communist Revolution in Russia in 1917 created a "Red Scare" in America which led to a distrust of foreigners and a questioning of the loyalty of our alien population. The cry for a "return to normalcy" after the war seemed to many to mean a return to the days before masses of immigrants came to this country from southern and eastern Europe. There was concern that Europe, seriously damaged by the war, might try to "dump" its needy on us. The prevailing sentiment in the United States opposed resumption of immigration at peak prewar levels.

In 1917, a literacy requirement was added to our laws. It had been vetoed in 1897 by Grover Cleveland, in 1913 by William Howard Taft, and twice by Woodrow Wilson who called it a test of a person's educational experience rather than one's potential as a future citizen. Also in 1917, an "Asian Barred Zone" cut off immigration from most of Asia and the Pacific Islands. The literacy test did not, however, succeed in barring everyone else. People from other countries could read and write too! A more effective policy was called for.

In 1921, Congress for the first time set limits on the *numbers* of immigrants who could come. Previous legislation to restrict immigration, except that banning Asians, attempted to control the quality of the immigrants. The 1921 law controlled the quantity . . . and the source.

NATIONAL ORIGINS
QUOTAS

The limit was set at about 350,000 people based on immigration quotas which allotted each country 3 percent of the foreign-born persons of that nationality living in the United States in 1910. Northern and western Europe received quotas totaling nearly 200,000, about 20,000 more than they had been averaging. Immigration from southern and eastern Europe was cut to a quota of 158,000, less than a quarter of its prewar average of 686,000.

An act of 1924 limited southern and eastern Europeans still further by using the base year of 1890 and a national origins quota system determined by country of birth or descent. Setting the quota at 2 percent reduced the total number of immigrants to 165,000, less than a fifth of the average prewar level. Northern and western Europe received 82 percent of the quotas. Only 23,000 came from all southern and eastern Europe. Italy was cut from 42,057 to 3,845; Poland, from 39,977 to 5,982; Turkey, from 2,654 to 100. A quota of 100 was common for most southern and eastern European countries. There were no quotas for countries of the Asian Barred Zone.

Beginning in 1929, the base year was set at 1920 and the ceiling at 150,000.

The national origins quota system, under which our immigration policy was not only restrictive but nationally biased and racist, remained in effect until 1968.

The quota policy marked the end of free mass migration to the United States. The 1924 Act not only checked the volume of immigration but limited the ethnic diversity by selecting those people considered the most "suitable" for American society. Abraham Lincoln had feared a Nativist policy which would declare that "All men are created equal, except Negroes, and foreigners, and Catholics." It now seemed that his fears had been realized.

In the twenty years between World War I and II, immigration to the United States was 68 percent less than the previous twenty-year period. Between 1901 and 1920, 14,531,197 immigrants entered; between 1920 and 1940, only 4,635,640 came.

During the Great Depression many quotas went unfilled. In the decade 1931–40, only 528,431 people came, hitting bottom in 1933 with 23,000. Between 1931 and 1936, 270,000 more people left the country than came here. During the depression, both Presidents Hoover and Roosevelt strictly enforced restrictions against people who might become public charges. It seemed to some that only rich Europeans were allowed to come.

NONQUOTA IMMIGRANTS

The 1921 Act established nonquota categories of immigrants. They included aliens returning from abroad, professional actors, artists, lecturers, nurses, ministers, and professors.

The 1924 Act extended the nonquota list to include those born in the western hemisphere, their wives and children; wives and children of United States citizens; clergymen and their families; former United States citizens; and domestic servants.

Nonquota immigration also dropped during the '30s, from an average 125,000 to 18,000 a year. Canadian immigration dropped from 75,000 to 13,000; Mexican immigration fell even more, from 50,000 to 3,000. Three times as many Mexicans left the country as entered, indicating that immigration across the border is primarily economic, rising and falling with the business cycle. In times of recession, when jobs are scarce, immigrants stay away.

WORLD WAR II

The rise of totalitarianism prevented many people from emigrating. Hitler and Mussolini considered it a national disgrace and discouraged it. So did Communist Russia.

The United States itself was so isolationist before the war that, as late as 1939, a proposal to admit 20,000 Jewish refugee children from Nazi Germany failed to pass Congress on the grounds that the German quota would be exceeded. In 1941, an Act authorized the refusal of visas to people considered a threat to the "public safety" and allowed the president to deport any alien "in the interests of the United States."

World War II changed the United States from isolationism to internationalism. Americans served in countries all over the world. American armies were integrated for the first time: blacks, American Indians, and Mexican-Americans served beside descendants of the "old" immigration and children of the "new." We numbered Russians, Chinese, Indians, Turks, Greeks, Poles, Africans, and Rumanians among our allies. We could hardly consider our allies undesirable aliens.

Congress repealed the ban on Chinese immigration in 1943, allowing 105 to enter each year and making them eligible for citizenship. In 1946, eligibility for naturalization was extended to people from India. The Philippine Islands were granted a quota of 100.

The shift from domestic to international concerns, which the war accelerated, led to a liberalization of immigration policy. World War II also increased presidential power. Immigration increasingly became an instrument of foreign policy under the president's control, particularly in dealing with war refugees.

THE COLD WAR AND THE
MCCARRAN-WALTER ACT

As Communism grew in strength and influence after World War II, anti-Communist and anti-foreign fears revived. In 1940, aliens were required to register annually and the Immigration and Naturalization Service (INS) was transferred

from the Department of Labor to the Department of Justice. In 1950, the Internal Security Act authorized exclusion or deportation of aliens who had been members of Communist or "Communist-front" organizations.

Under such leadership as that of Senator Joseph McCarthy, who warned of "subversives" and "un-American" forces, Congress passed the McCarran-Walter Immigration and Nationality Act of 1952, the first major immigration legislation since 1924. Although the act extended the right of entry to Asians, it set a ceiling of 150,000 on eastern hemisphere immigration and retained the discriminatory national origins system based on the 1920 census. This prompted President Harry Truman to state in his veto message:

> *The idea behind this discriminatory policy was, to put it baldly, that Americans with English or Irish names were better people and better citizens than Americans with Italian, or Greek, or Polish names. It was thought that people of western European origin made better citizens than Rumanians, or Yugoslavs, or Ukrainians, or Balts, or Austrians. Such a concept is utterly unworthy of our traditions and our ideals.*
>
> *. . . It is incredible to me that in this year of 1952, we should again be enacting into law such a slur on the patriotism, the capacity, and the decency of a large part of our citizenry.*

Senator Patrick McCarran warned of "hard-core indigestible blocks which have not become integrated into the American way of life" and defended his bill, stating that it was:

> *. . . tough, very tough, on Communists, as it is on criminals and other subversives, and that is why they are squealing. It is a tragic fact that the out-and-out Reds have ready colleagues in this fight: The "Pinks," the well-meaning but misguided "liberals" and the demagogues*

**Postwar refugees arrive
in the United States.**

who would auction the interests of America for alleged minority-bloc votes.

Congress, often a foe of liberal immigration in the past and anxious to retain control over it in the future, passed the Act over Truman's veto. The McCarran-Walter Act assigned 85 percent of Europe's quotas to northern and western Europe.

To ensure the stability of the desired national ethnic mix, refugees, when admitted, were "mortgaged" or deducted from future quotas. At one time, Latvia's quota was mortgaged until the year 2274; Greece, until 2013; Poland, until 1999; and Rumania, until 2001.

The Act also introduced preference categories under which immigrants were granted entry. Fifty percent of all immigrant visas were set aside for relatives of citizens and resident aliens (the "family reunification" principle which is at the heart of United States immigration policy today). Another 50 percent went to skilled workers and others with special education and technical training who might make a contribution to the national economy. If any category went unfilled, others could come. The Act enlarged the nonquota class to include immediate relatives of citizens and permanent resident aliens alike.

THE END OF
NATIONAL ORIGINS

The McCarran-Walter Act is still in effect although the national origins quota system was abolished by the Amendments of 1965 which were introduced by President Kennedy (grandson of an Irish immigrant and the first Catholic president) and passed under President Lyndon B. Johnson. Also abolished was the Asia-Pacific triangle as an area of ineligibility. A ceiling of 170,000, with a per country limit of 20,000, was placed on immigration from the eastern hemisphere.

The preference system was expanded to seven categories: 74 percent of visa allocations favored family reunification for relatives of citizens and permanent resident aliens; 10 percent favored professionals and people of exceptional ability in the sciences and arts who would benefit the national economy, culture, or welfare; and another 10 percent, skilled and unskilled workers in short supply who would not take jobs from citizens or legal alien workers. The remaining 6 percent was allotted to refugees from Communist or Communist-dominated countries, the Middle East, or areas struck by natural disaster. If the seven preference categories were not filled, other potential immigrants might apply.

The effects of abolishing the national origins quota system are striking: China, which sent a total of 1,000 per year between 1955 and 1965, sent 9,000 in 1975; India, 300 in 1965, 14,000 in 1975; Greece, 4,400 in 1965, 9,800 in 1975; Portugal, 2,200 in 1965 and 11,000 in 1975. Between 1920 and 1960, Europe accounted for 60 percent of all United States immigration; Central and South America, 35 percent; Asia, 3 percent. In 1975, Europe sent 19 percent; Central and South America, 43 percent; and Asia, 34 percent.

RESTRICTING THE WESTERN HEMISPHERE

Before 1965, no quotas were set for immigrants from the western hemisphere, in keeping with our "Good Neighbor" policy. However, between 1945 and 1965, over 1.3 million Mexicans came to this country as resident aliens. An additional 5 million entered between 1942 and 1964 as part of a "bracero" (day laborer) program providing temporary (and cheap) labor for the farms and expanding industries of California and the Southwest. Not everyone went home.

Some Hispanics have been in the U.S. longer than many Americans. There were 75,000 Mexicans living in the lands of the Southwest before the Mexican-American War (1846–48). Many Mexicans do not recognize the Treaty of Guadalupe-Hidalgo, which ended the war, set the present boundaries, and ceded two-fifths of Mexico's territory to the United States. Many Mexicans felt that they had a long-established right to move freely back and forth across the border. Many still do.

With the Amendments of 1965, Congress traded the national origins quota system for a ceiling of 120,000 on the western hemisphere. In 1976, the preference system and the 20,000-per-country limit were extended to the west; and, in 1978, the totals of the two hemispheres were combined into a worldwide ceiling of 290,000.

In spite of worldwide ceilings, immigration continued to soar: 502,000 in 1978, 526,000 in 1979, 808,000 in 1980, and an estimated 697,000 in 1981. Husbands, wives, and minor children of citizens; parents of adult citizens; and refugees admitted under parole by the Attorney General are exempt from numerical ceilings. They accounted for 189,000 people in 1978, 270,000 in 1979, and 506,000 in 1980.

In addition, untold numbers entered the United States illegally, leading many authorities to believe that, in reality, our annual rate of immigration is closer to one million. This would equal the all-time-high rates at the beginning of the century.

In 1978, Congress established a Select Commission on Immigration and Refugee Policy to study a system many felt was just not working.

O! receive the fugitive, and prepare
in time an asylum for mankind.
                              Thomas Paine

The rest of the world should stop
dumping their garbage on our shores.
                              Fay Douglas
                   Taxpayers Revolt Association
                              Los Angeles

REFUGEES

When the Great Wave of Immigration ended, the Age of the Refugee began. There may be 16 million refugees in the world today: Afghans in Pakistan; Cambodians in Thailand; Palestinians in Jordan, Lebanon, and Syria. Four and a half million Africans, including nearly a million ethnic Somalis from the Ogaden region of Ethiopia and another million Eritreans, are refugees. People are in flight from Bulgaria, Chile, Cuba, Cyprus, Haiti, Laos, North Korea, Pakistan, Tibet, the Soviet Union, and Vietnam. As the population of the world increases, perhaps to 6 billion by the year 2000, the number of refugees will undoubtedly increase too.

There were refugees in other times: among them, Jews and Moors expelled from Spain in the late fifteenth century; people who fled from religious persecution to the United States in the sixteenth and seventeenth centuries; European revolutionaries and Jews fleeing pogroms in Russia in the nineteenth century. It was not until the twentieth century, however, that

[35

refugees came to be recognized as an international concern, distinguished by law from other groups of immigrants.

Unlike other immigrants, refugees do not migrate primarily in search of the opportunities offered by an expanding country or a growing economy. They are political fugitives whose status creates legal problems as well as humanitarian concerns.

The first refugees of our century were 1.5 million "White" Russians fleeing the Revolution of 1917. German and Russian prisoners required repatriation after World War I. Many Bulgarians left their homes and Greeks and Armenians fled from Turkey.

In 1921, in an attempt to deal with problems like these, the League of Nations appointed the noted Norwegian explorer Fridtjof Nansen High Commissioner for Refugees. The International Labor Organization (ILO) later assisted in this work. Special passports, recognized by as many as fifty-four countries in some circumstances, gave refugees safe conduct across national borders.

The rise to power of Adolf Hitler in Germany, followed by the annexation of Austria and Czechoslovakia, and the growth of anti-Semitism in Europe created many refugees. After the Loyalist defeat in Spain in 1939, 340,000 Spaniards fled to southern France.

At the suggestion of President Roosevelt, thirty-two governments met in France in 1938 to create an Inter-Governmental Committee on Refugees. Some progress was made, but concern for relations with Germany prevented much action. Many refugees were forced to return to their countries of origin, where they were often forbidden to work or imprisoned.

The end of World War II magnified the refugee problem. An estimated 50 million people migrated after the war. Many had been forcibly removed from their homes as prisoners of war or slave laborers or had become exiles for racial or political reasons. They were given the name "displaced persons (DPs)." In five months after Germany's surrender, 7 million DPs were repatriated by the United Nations Relief and Rehabilitation Administration (UNRRA). The United States contributed half of UNRRA's $4 billion budget, made up of 2 percent of the national incomes of fifty-two countries.

Another million people did not want to go home again. They included Germans, Austrians, and Italians who were outside their homelands because of prewar fascist persecution or postwar changes of government. Germans streaming out of East Germany, eventually totaling 12 million, were left to the responsibility of the West German government. Other eastern Europeans, fleeing to the West at the rate of 1,000 to 1,500 a month, created an additional million "new" refugees. Many Jews sought homes in Palestine; over the next thirty years, 8 million Jews migrated to Israel.

In 1946, the United Nations recognized refugees as an ongoing problem and set up the International Refugee Organization (IRO) to deal with them. Over the next five years, the IRO repatriated 73,000 and resettled nearly a million people.

The United Nations Universal Declaration of Human Rights of 1948 stated: "Everyone has the right to seek and to enjoy in other countries asylum from persecution. . . ." The right to asylum is the refugee's right to life.

Unrest around the world continued to create masses of refugees. The partition of India in 1947 created 10 million refugees. After the founding of Israel in 1948, over 770,000 Palestinians fled to other countries. Many Chinese left the mainland and flooded into Hong Kong and Taiwan after the Communist victory in China in 1949. The Korean War (1950–53) created another 9 million refugees.

Since the IRO dealt only with European refugees, the UN sought individual solutions to problems in other areas of the world: the United Nations Relief and Works Agency (UNRWA) for the Palestinians and the United Nations Korean Reconstruction Agency (UNKRA) for Korea were two of the agencies set up. Hong Kong designated refugees as immigrants, which meant they were not eligible for UN programs. In many cases, private organizations and British and United States agencies took over their care.

In 1951, the Office of the United Nations High Commissioner for Refugees (UNHCR) was created to provide legal protection for refugees all over the world and to see that governments everywhere met their obligations toward them. Its responsibilities grew to include assistance in financing transportation, resettlement, food, shelter, and health care. Through another agency, the Inter-Governmental Committee for European Migration (ICEM), UNHCR has attempted to relieve population pressures in Europe and Southeast Asia by aiding emigration from troubled areas to more stable countries of permanent asylum.

In 1954, the UN Convention Relating to the Status of Refugees, or the "Refugee Magna Carta," went into effect. It defined refugees as persons who are outside their homelands because of fear of persecution for race, religion, nationality, political opinion, or membership in a particular social group and who are unable or unwilling, because of that fear, to return to their country of origin or seek its protection. The Convention guaranteed that refugees would not be penalized for illegal entry nor expelled to "the frontiers of territories" where their life or freedom would be threatened.

The Convention also defined the legal rights of refugees. In matters of religion, public education, social security, and public welfare, refugees were to enjoy the same rights as nationals of the country to which they fled. In matters of employment, property rights, access to housing and higher education, professional standing, and advanced training, they were to realize the same rights as all other aliens. Travel documents became the responsibility of the adoptive country.

The Convention defined refugee status as of January 1, 1951 and applied it only to Europe. Events in Hungary after 1954 and in Africa during the fifties and sixties produced many additional refugees who did not meet the Convention's criteria. In 1967, the UN Protocol Relating to the Status of Refugees brought the Convention up to date and extended its benefits around the world. The Declaration of Territorial Asylum stated that "no person . . . shall be subjected to rejection at the frontier or . . . expulsion or compulsory return to any state where [they] may be subjected to persecution."

The UNHCR continues to coordinate international activities in aid of refugees, with the voluntary cooperation of national, international, and private agencies, organizations, and groups.

REFUGEES IN
THE UNITED STATES

George Washington hoped that our country would always be "an asylum for the oppressed and needy of the earth." Many of our first settlers were refugees.

In our time, the United States has been the strongest supporter of United Nations refugee programs and has acted on its own in the aid of refugees from eastern Europe, Africa, South Vietnam, Cambodia, Laos, and Cuba and Chinese refugees in Hong Kong and Macao. In 1980 alone, 350,000 refugees entered the United States. An additional 135,000 became eligible for citizenship. American expenditures for refugee programs totaled nearly $4 billion.

Since the close of World War II, the United States has received over 1 million refugees, more than any other country in the world. (Canada and Australia have been receptive to refugees too; although Canada at one time specified that they do heavy labor and Australia demanded a two-year work contract and gave special preference to single males from Baltic states. France has received large numbers of Indochinese refugees.)

THE BRAIN DRAIN

Hitler's rise to power in Germany in 1933, the development of anti-Semitism in Italy after 1938, and the fall of France in 1940 were some of the events which led to the mass exodus from Europe of teachers, scholars, scientists, and other intellectuals, irreverently dubbed the "brain drain." It is estimated that as many as 25,000 of them came to the United States between 1933 and 1944.

Like all immigrants, they were greeted with mixed emotions. When Albert Einstein decided to emigrate in 1932, some people opposed his entry here, called him a German Bolshevist, and stated that his theory "was of no scientific value or purpose, not understandable because there was nothing there to understand."

However, many organizations worked to find sponsors, homes, and jobs for the gifted newcomers whose contributions enriched American culture and furthered the growth of American science.

Among the famous immigrants who came during this period were: artists Josef and Anni Albers and Max Ernst (Germany), Marc Chagall (Russia); musicians Bela Bartok (Hungary), Bruno Walter (Germany), José Iturbi (Spain), Arturo Toscanini (Italy), Vladimir Horowitz (Russia); writers Bertolt Brecht, Erich Fromm, and Thomas Mann (Germany); architects Mies Van der Rohe (Germany), Marcel Breuer (Hungary); theologian Paul Tillich (Germany); psychologist Bruno Bettelheim (Austria); political scientist Hannah Arendt (Germany); and physicists Niels Bohr (Denmark), Enrico Fermi (Italy), and Edward Teller (Hungary), whose work led to the development of the atomic bomb.

POSTWAR POLICY

Until 1965, there was no legal provision for admitting refugees to the United States in large numbers. Entry was governed by national quotas under the immigration Act of 1924 and, later, the McCarran-Walter Act of 1952.

In 1945, President Truman used his authority to admit some 40,000 Poles, Balts, and southern Europeans, charging them to quota numbers which had accumulated during the war. He also pressed Congress to pass the "War Brides Act," admitting 120,000 foreign-born husbands, wives, and children of members of the U.S. Armed Forces, mostly from Great Britain, Ireland, Germany, Italy, Canada, Australia, and New Zealand. Special exceptions were made for Europeans stranded in the Far East after the war and for 20,000 war orphans from Germany, Italy, Greece, Japan, Korea, and other countries.

The Displaced Persons Act of 1948, adopted at Truman's urging over strong opposition in Congress, provided for admission of 400,000 refugees over four years, charged to future quotas. Three quarters of these DPs came from countries with low quotas such as Greece, Italy, Latvia, Poland, USSR, and Yugoslavia. One quarter were Germans. At first, the legislation proved to be discriminatory against Catholics and Jews; it was later revised to correct this.

Under the Refugee Relief Act of 1953, the United States for the first time ignored the quota system and granted visas to some 5,000 Hungarians who had fled their country after an anti-Communist revolution failed. During President Eisenhower's term, 30,000 more were allowed to enter "on parole," a clause of the McCarran-Walter Act which granted the Attorney General the right to admit any alien for "emergency reasons," including the national interest. The parole authority has also been used to admit 90,000 Jews from Soviet Russia.

In all, between 1953 and 1958, over 200,000 Europeans and Chinese were admitted without quota restrictions under the Refugee Relief Act.

Between 1952 and 1961, the U.S. Escapee Program (USEP) helped relocate 600,000 escapees from Communism, mostly from eastern Europe.

Mortgages on quotas were discontinued in 1957 and unused visas distributed to refugees, expellees, and their families. Nonquota admission was granted in 1957 to Hollanders expelled from Indonesia and in 1958 to Portuguese in the Azores who had been displaced by earthquake and floods. In 1959, close relatives of refugees were admitted. After the Castro Revolution in Cuba, many Cubans were admitted by parole under the "Fair Share" Refugee Act of 1960.

In 1965, the Amendments to the McCarran-Walter Act recognized refugees as a separate group of immigrants and listed them as the seventh preference category, eligible for 6 percent of the annual ceiling (17,400 places in 1978). They were given the right to apply for permanent resident, or immigrant, status after two years.

The U.S. law defined refugees as persons who had fled from any Communist or Communist-dominated country or area, or from any country in the general area of the Middle East. As a result of the quota limitation and the restriction on the country of origin, most of the huge numbers of refugees who entered the United States between 1965 and 1980 came as parolees rather than under the preference category.

INDOCHINESE

After a long and bitter war in Vietnam, Saigon fell to the North Vietnamese Army in April 1975. Almost immediately, over a hundred thousand Vietnamese (including a group of 2,000 orphans), 5,000 Cambodians, and some Laotians boarded U.S. ships and planes and were paroled into the United States. Temporary asylum was granted for processing on Guam. In the United States, an interagency task force was set up at reception centers in Arkansas, California, Florida, and Pennsylvania. Private voluntary organizations, many of them church groups, found sponsors for immigrants without family ties, arranged transportation, and helped them find homes and jobs, take English lessons, and learn to become self-supporting. One hundred thirty thousand refugees were resettled in eight months, an impressive achievement.

The flight from racial persecution, political chaos, famine, and repressive governments in Indochina continues. "Land" people come from Cambodia and Laos and cross into Thailand. There have been 450,000 of them. The invasion of Cambodia by the Vietnamese in the fall of 1979 created an additional 300,000 Cambodian refugees. Many people remain in refugee camps in Thailand. Others are in hiding along the border. Thirty thousand Vietnamese and 260,000 ethnic Chinese, expelled from their homes in Vietnam, crossed into China. (Many of them wished to settle elsewhere, but after six-months' residence they are no longer considered refugees and, hence, are not eligible for resettlement.)

From Vietnam came the "boat" people, perhaps as many as 370,000, braving the waters of the South China Sea in rickety wooden boats and fishing vessels. Boat captains are required by international law to help these people but, as their numbers grew, many captains ignored them. Other refugees were subject to murder, rape, and robbery by Thai sea pirates. Some estimates say as many as 30 percent of the boat people perished.

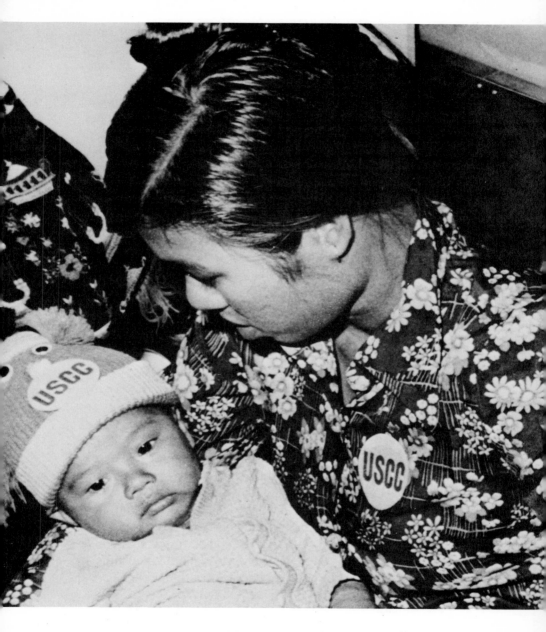

In San Francisco, a Vietnamese mother and her child, admitted under a special program, begin a new life.

Some boat people sailed as far as Australia, 2,000 miles away. A few big boats went into Hong Kong and Manila Bay. But most of the boat people landed in Malaysia and Indonesia.

Thailand and Malaysia have been hostile to the Vietnamese. As boats put into Singapore, Hong Kong, the Philippines, and Indonesia, those overpopulated countries found it difficult to support the refugees who descended on them. At best, they were willing to grant temporary asylum. Some land people have been turned away at the borders. Some boat people, refused permission to go ashore, have been towed back out to sea.

The major task of resettlement rests with the UNHCR and ICEM. After an international conference in 1978, seventy-two countries pledged to help with monetary contributions, temporary processing centers, transportation to countries of permanent asylum, and interim food, shelter, and health care. An agreement on orderly departure from Vietnam was arranged. But the political problems which create refugees in Indochina remain.

INDOCHINESE IN
THE UNITED STATES

Since 1975, 428,000 Indochinese have settled in the United States, arriving at the rate of 14,000 a month in 1980. The number was expected to reach 600,000 by 1982. Seventy-eight percent of the refugees are Vietnamese; 17 percent, Laotians; 5 percent, Cambodians.

The "latecomers"—to distinguish them from the "old" and "new" immigration—are again changing the faces of our cities and towns. New York now has an Asian-American population of 400,000; Los Angeles has over 100,000 Indochinese; Houston, 25,000. Many Vietnamese have settled in Texas, where the climate is most like home.

Vietnamese, Koreans, and other Indochinese are highly industrious. The whole family works and they often take several jobs in bars and restaurants, small factories, garment centers, grocery stores and supermarkets. They save until they are able to open their own restaurants or fruit stands or flower shops or fish markets. They help feed themselves with their own vegetable gardens. They crowd together in shacks and tenement apartments until they can afford their own homes. They sacrifice to send their children to school and college.

Inevitably, there have been confrontations between the Indochinese and other ethnic groups. One person was murdered in a dispute over fishing rights in Texas. In California, some Indochinese were apprehended in the public parks for hunting wildlife and gathering flowers, berries, and shrubs for food.

The Indochinese are hampered by the language barrier, cultural differences, and lack of representation on police forces and in other local organizations.

"It's a subtle culture," said a Los Angeles policeman. "We probably will never get a handle on it, not in this generation."

More than any other immigrants, refugees need to feel they are accepted. "We can talk about concepts like 'acculturation' and 'assimilation,'" says one spokesman, "and provide money and programs to set refugees on their feet. But what refugees need most of all is acceptance and a feeling of being welcomed."

Meanwhile, the latecomers try to adjust. One Vietnamese told the *New York Times,* "I don't know the United States life, but I know it is what we want. But first I must work hard, get money, get English."

REFUGEE ACT
OF 1980

The Refugee Act of 1980, the first major reform of immigration law since 1965, attempted to bring legislative policy in line with current events. It defined as a refugee any person forced to leave his or her country because of persecution on account of race, religion, nationality, political opinion, or membership in a social group in any part of the world. This eliminated the geographical and ideological restrictions of the past and brought our definition in line with that of the UN Protocol. The new law also made it easier for refugees to apply for entry to the United States.

This meant that many groups who had been restricted in the past could now apply, including Afghans, Eritreans, Somalis, South Africans, Namibians, Ugandans, Libyans, and others who face the "risk of persecution" in parts of Asia and Africa.

The "normal flow" of refugees to be admitted in any one year was raised from 17,400 to 50,000, with the President deciding which groups to admit and having the right, in consultation with Congress, to increase the limit under conditions of "special humanitarian concern" to the United States.

The Act assured to every refugee uniform federal funding for a maximum of three years through grants to voluntary, state, and local agencies and public assistance programs. An Office of Refugee Resettlement was established in the Department of Health and Human Services to administer the funds.

An Office of Refugee Coordinator in the Department of State was made responsible for developing admissions and resettlement policy, coordinating domestic and international programs, and recommending a budget. The office serves as liaison with other government and international agencies, voluntary agencies, and local authorities. The Coordinator is charged with developing recommendations in four problem areas: orientation and acculturation; housing; job training and placement; and public affairs and community tensions.

The Departments of Labor and Health and Social Services are to work together to find areas where labor shortages exist and to encourage refugee settlement there.

Voluntary agencies remain largely responsible for refugee placement. In making their decisions, they consider location of other family members, personal preference, and availability of local sponsors.

The ink was barely dry on the new law when President Carter authorized the entry of 228,000 refugees, many more than the 50,000 proposed by the Act. Before the year's end, an additional 136,000 unexpected arrivals made a mockery of the original estimates.

CUBANS

In April 1980, when guards were temporarily removed from the Peruvian Embassy in Havana, 10,000 Cubans stormed the grounds and requested asylum. The United States agreed to take 3,500 of the refugees in addition to its authorized 1980 Cuban quota of 16,000. Peru agreed to take 1,000; Spain, 500; Costa Rica and Canada, 300; Ecuador, 200. Seven hundred people were granted exit visas and flown from Cuba to Costa Rica, designated the country of first asylum, for further processing and transportation to countries of permanent asylum. Then, suddenly, Castro canceled the airlift and the sealift to the United States began.

Friends and relatives crowded into Key West in south Florida to hire lobster and shrimp boats, yachts, and motorboats of all shapes and sizes for the 110-mile (177-km) journey across the Florida Straits, to the port of Mariel in Cuba, to pick up the refugees and bring them to America. Boat captains pocketed anywhere from $1,000 to $1,500 per passenger (payable in advance). A few charged nothing. Many encountered rough seas, 15-foot- (4.6-m) high waves, and 25-mile- (40-km) per-hour winds on the trip.

By the time the "Freedom Flotilla" was called off in September, when Castro closed the port, 125,000 Cubans had arrived at our doorstep. They presented us with a problem we had almost never known before: large numbers of refugees landing directly on our shores. The new refugee law hadn't foreseen that.

Nearly all previous refugees had applied for entry visas to the United States from first sites of asylum elsewhere. The 155,000 Cubans who entered after the overthrow of Batista in 1959 and the 265,000 who came here under authorization of President Johnson between 1965 and 1973 made the trip in orderly "freedom flights." The masses of Indochinese who entered after 1975 were preprocessed, screened, and documented before they crossed the Pacific.

Called into action for the emergency in Florida were representatives of the Departments of State (Coordinator for Refugee Affairs), Justice (INS), Labor, Education, Health and Social Services (Office of Refugee Resettlement), the Coast Guard, Customs Service, Federal Emergency Management Agency, National Guard, state and local agencies, numerous voluntary organizations, the FBI, the CIA, and the Marines. Border Patrol agents were transferred from duty along the Mexican border.

A state of emergency was declared in Key West and Miami. Cots were set up under the Miami thruway, in airplane hangars and missile bases, and even in the Orange Bowl. A second processing center was established at Eglin Air Force Base in northwest Florida and others, later, in Arkansas, Pennsylvania, and Wisconsin. Cuban communities all over the country donated food, clothing, funds, and sponsorship. Catholic refugee services resettled about 70 percent of the Cubans. Homosexual-rights groups helped resettle some 5,000 homosexuals.

Meanwhile, billboards in Havana blazed, "Let the scum leave," and the departing Cubans were branded as "escoria" (trash) and "gusanos" (worms or parasites), "antisocial" and "antirevolutionary" elements, and traitors. Boats were forced to take Cubans the government wished to expel, including about 2,750 criminals and mental defectives, in addition to the fugitives in the Peruvian Embassy and relatives of Cuban-Americans.

The U.S. government wavered between trying to contain the exodus by threatening to seize the boats or fine their owners and trying to make the best of events it could not control. Cubans who were immediate relatives of U.S. citizens and resident aliens were, when documented, eligible to enter under routine immigration law. Castro did not seem willing to cooperate in accepting the return of others. Some of the outflow probably helped ease Cuba's unemployment problems. Furthermore, under the UN Protocol of 1967, which the United States signed, we could not turn away bona fide refugees. Besides, we had a twenty-year history of welcoming Cubans who were fleeing a Communist regime which we did not recognize.

In May, President Carter announced that we would "provide an open heart and open minds" to the new Cuban refugees and, later, with 11,000 Haitians who had also fled to south Florida during the year, they were admitted "condi-

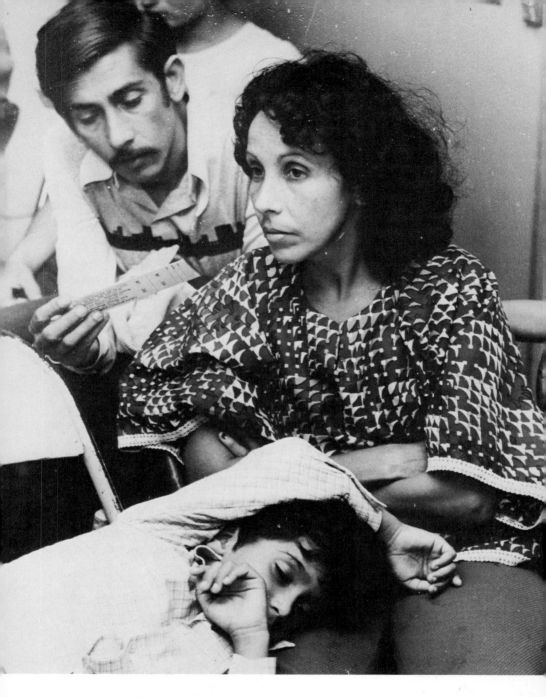

Cuban refugees wait for immigration clearance in Key West during the 1980 "shuttle."

tionally," as "entrants," for six months, until Congress could determine their legal standing. The President said the federal government would help pay resettlement costs, health screening and education costs. The "entrants" were made eligible for federally subsidized social programs (as other immigrants are), including food stamps but not welfare, as many mistakenly believed. The federal government authorized $100 million in general assistance and medical aid. Ninety percent of the refugees were found to have relatives in the United States. Although there were incidents of violence in some of the camps and complaints that the resettlement process was slow and unwieldy, all but 10,000 of the Cubans were resettled in less than six months, equaling the Indochinese record.

Before the influx of 1980, there were about 700,000 Cubans in the United States. Over half of them lived in metropolitan Miami (Dade County), Florida. Most of the newcomers wanted to live there, too. Miami was faced with the monumental task of trying to absorb nearly 100,000 of them.

Schools went into double session, hospitals became overcrowded, and jails overflowed. The crime rate went up 124 percent for robbery; 109 percent for assault; 60 percent for car theft; and 103 percent for homicide.

The county school board said it could not afford the special counseling needed to help the refugees adjust to American life or the classes in math and social studies it was required to teach in Spanish (and in Creole, as well, for Haitian refugees). The board estimated the 20,000 school-age children expected to register in the fall would cost the county $20 million.

A county commissioner threw up his hands and stated angrily, "Everybody can't live in Dade County!" But Miami is well on its way to becoming the first major U.S. city with a Hispanic majority.

Most people thought that eventually the new refugees would benefit Miami. "In our state, more people means more money," said a Florida economics professor. Between 1960 and 1969, federal support for Cuban refugees totaled $1.3 billion and helped bolster Miami's economy. The city's unemployment rate is below the national average; retail stores thrive; and Miami attracts large numbers of Latin American tourists and investors. The first wave of Cubans fleeing the Castro revolution are generally credited with transforming the city into the bustling bilingual, bicultural, international community it is today.

The first wave of Cubans in 1959 consisted largely of well-educated members of the middle class, however. The second wave was largely young and unskilled, although many did have a trade. Most of them were expected to take positions at low wages at the bottom of the economic scale, in hotels, agriculture, and the garment industry. This meant they would compete for scarce housing, jobs, and health care not only with Miami's disadvantaged blacks but with another group of latecomers, the Haitians.

HAITIANS

Haiti is the poorest nation in the western hemisphere: annual income is about $130; illiteracy, 87 percent; and half the people are unemployed. It is, in addition, burdened with the repressive regime of President-for-Life Jean Claude ("Baby Doc") Duvalier, a non-Communist government which the United States supports.

Haitians took to the boats in 1972; by the end of 1980, there were an estimated 40,000 of them seeking refuge in south Florida. Officially, there are fewer than 100,000 Haitians in the country; unofficially, as many as 300,000 to 500,000 may be here illegally. They have settled largely in New York City, Washington, Boston, and Chicago.

Haitians speak neither English nor Spanish, but Creole, a mixture of English, French, Spanish, and African dialects. In addition, many of them practice Voodoo, which sets them apart from Afro-American and Hispanic communities as well as from whites.

The Haitians in Florida requested political asylum. The Immigration and Naturalization Service seldom granted their requests, holding that Haitians were "economic refugees" without a "well-grounded fear of persecution" if they were to return to their country. They were, more often, ordered jailed and deported. Classified as illegal aliens, Haitians were denied work permits or federal assistance. Poor, without proper housing, mostly illiterate, they could not apply for federal aid (although a Haitian child born here would qualify for food stamps).

Some groups, including Amnesty International and the National Council of Churches, claimed evidence of arrests, torture, beatings, and unexplained disappearances of Haitians who were deported to their homeland. Others, including representatives of the State Department, said no such signs of political reprisals existed.

In July 1980, in a class-action suit brought by 4,000 Haitians, a federal district judge in Florida found that the INS had violated the rights of Haitians, denying them due process in its eagerness to process them quickly and deport them.

The judge found that the service had been motivated in some degree by racial bias and noted that the Haitians were "part of the first substantial flight of black refugees from a repressive regime to this country." (President Carter's "open arms" welcome for the Cubans did not at first seem to embrace the Haitians.)

"Haitians who came to the United States seeking freedom and justice did not find it," said the judge who stated that each request for asylum must be considered individually on its merits. He further stated that the INS had failed to grasp "the fundamental rules of Haitian politics and economics," that the country's "dramatic poverty" was largely "a result of Duvalier's efforts to maintain power," making economics and politics hard to distinguish.

The Haitians eventually won a reprieve from President Carter. In June 1980 he granted the Haitians, along with the Cubans, the right to six-months' temporary residence until Congress should pass legislation allowing them to become permanent resident aliens and, eventually, citizens.

By year's end, Miamians felt they were bearing more than their share of the burden of the new Cuban and Haitian refugees who had descended on them as a result—or lack—of national policy. The federal government promised an additional $2,000 per refugee to help private agencies with resettlement.

While this solved some immediate problems for Miami, many questions remained unanswered, among them: Is it fair to open our arms to Cuba and Haiti and to expel our economically deprived Mexican neighbors? How do we deal with persons who may not have had a "well-founded fear of persecution" before they left home, but fear to return? What do we do with expellees whom we don't want but the sending country won't take back?

President Carter welcomed "refugees seeking freedom from Communist domination and from economic deprivation brought about by Fidel Castro and his government." A federal judge suggested that economic deprivation caused by right-wing political repression was also grounds for asylum. Other governments in South America may be guilty of repression and persecution. "If the Haitians can stay, the whole hemisphere is eligible," said one government lawyer. "The U.S. cannot become a place of residence for everyone who wants to come here," said another.

To all appearances, the refugee problem is with us to stay. The number of refugees authorized for 1981 was 217,000, only 14,700 fewer than 1980. It was to include 168,000 Indochinese; 37,500 refugees from the USSR and eastern Europe; 4,500 from the Near East; 3,000 from Africa. Latin America was reduced from a quota of 20,500 to 4,000 (as a result of the Cuban sealift). The refugee program was estimated to cost the United States $690 million. Many Americans felt a cutback was in order.

Theodore M. Hesburgh, chairman of the government's Select Commission on Immigration and Refugee Policy, asked, "How does a country founded on a revolutionary belief in human rights and a concern for human potential decide which and how many refugees to receive, knowing that some limits must be imposed?"

ILLEGALS

They crowd into small boats bound for Florida and Puerto Rico. They cut through fences, or burrow under them, or ford the shallow waters of the Rio Grande along the 2,000-mile Mexican border. Under cover of darkness, they come across from Canada, where the border is largely unguarded. They drown. They lose their way and die of dehydration in the desert. Hiding inside ballast tanks on a smuggling ship, they are asphyxiated. Sometimes they are shot. But many of them make it.

They are the illegal aliens, officially known as "undocumented persons." What to do about them is the major immigration issue facing us today.

Those who run the border are known as EWIs (*entered without inspection*). They account for about 80 percent. Others are "visa abusers" or "overstayers" who enter legally as students, visitors, or tourists, and never go home. The INS

[54

lost track of 15 percent of the 9.3 million visitors to the United States in 1978; 42,300 foreign college students were unaccounted for. Still other illegals are "fraudulent entrants" who often pay a fortune for forged documents, including passports and visas, birth and marriage certificates, false bank statements, Social Security cards, driver's licenses, and job offers.

Nobody knows how many illegals there are. There is no way to count them. The INS located 1 million deportable aliens in 1977 and 1978; many others have slipped its grasp. Estimates on the number of illegals in the country range from 1 to 8 million. The Census Bureau in 1980 set the total below 6 million, maybe as low as 3.5 to 5 million, but some estimates run as high as 12 million. The Federation for American Immigration Reform (FAIR) put the annual increment at 800,000 to a million.

Many authorities think most illegals residing in the United States are Mexicans, although there is disagreement on that too. The Census Bureau says Mexicans are less than half the total, no more than 3 million, but 92 percent of all deportable aliens located in 1979 were Mexicans. Other illegals come from the Caribbean, Central and South America, Asia, and Europe.

Some Mexican illegals bring their wives and children and settle permanently in the United States, but others roam back and forth across the border in search of seasonal employment. Some commute to work daily. They can do this more freely than other groups since their homes are nearby. As a result, their *net* or permanent immigration may be lower than suspected.

Most Mexicans are EWIs. Non-Mexicans are more likely to be visa abusers or fraudulent entrants; although there are EWIs from Haiti, the Dominican Republic, and South America, as well as a few from Asia (especially the Philippines) and Africa. Many of them enter by way of Canada.

OTMs (INS designation for Other-Than-Mexicans) are not as free to respond to short-term changes in the U.S. economy, such as the availability of jobs, or seasonal employment. The cost of returning home is usually prohibitive.

**Captured illegals await
the return trip to Mexico.**

DEPORTABLE ALIENS LOCATED
BY NATIONALITY, 1978

Mexico	976,667
North America *(except Mexico)*	36,052
Asia	14,775
Europe	13,981
South America	10,801
Africa	2,910
Other	2,791

Most Mexican illegals settle in the Southwest, especially California and Texas. Other illegals head for the big cities of the eastern or midwestern states, particularly New York and Chicago, where there is already a varied mix of nationalities and their foreign dress and language do not stand out.

WHY THEY COME

Illegals—like other immigrants—come because, as Goethe said in another century, America still has it better than the world they left. There is a great gap between the economy of the United States and that of Third World countries, Mexico, and South America. Most illegals are of working age and looking for jobs. In some overpopulated Mexican border cities, half the labor force is idle. Immigrants can often make in a day here what it takes a week or more to earn at home—if jobs are available at all. Sometimes political unrest adds to economic problems: in the "troubled triangle" of Nicaragua, Guatemala, and El Salvador, for instance.

⯀ Many of the world's dissatisfied people are frustrated in their attempts to enter the United States legally. There is a five- to nine-year backlog of over a million persons waiting for visas at consular offices around the world; 700,000 of them are relatives of immigrants already here. In the Dominican Republic, where living standards are extremely low, 500 people apply for visas to the United States every day. Forty percent of them are rejected. They are poor and unskilled and their relatives here are seldom able to prove they can support them if they come. It is estimated that about 10 percent of the Dominican population now lives in New York City, about half of them illegally.

SMUGGLING

The business of smuggling aliens has become as profitable as running drugs. Marine wives, customs officers, Border Patrol agents, air traffic controllers, even Roman Catholic priests have been caught at it. Now organized crime is getting into the act. A big ring in El Paso reportedly grossed $10 million to $25 million in 1980. The average ring takes in about $38,000 a week. When the leader of a San Diego group was caught, she walked out on $250,000 bail.

Fees, payable in advance, average $300 for transport from the Mexican border to Denver; $500, to Chicago; $750, to New York City. A price of $3,000 from Santo Domingo to Miami via Panamanian freighter included forged documents (such as fake "green cards," the work permit required of aliens), new clothes, the promise of a job and a taxi to New York. In 1980, a Guatemalan travel agency charged $1,200 to smuggle Salvadorans and promised them a plane ride to Los Angeles after they crossed the Mexican–U.S. border. Instead, they died in a sunparched Arizona desert. Some smuggling rings specialize—in waiters or prostitutes for instance—and deliver on order. Some offer a second trip if the first one fails.

The United States apprehended 76,000 smuggled aliens in 1975; 211,000 in 1979. Two to five times as many may get through.

Smugglers call themselves "coyotes" and their alien customers "pollos" or "chickens." They travel in beer trucks, mobile homes, and moving vans, to shabby "drop houses" on the Mexican border and "wetback motels" in places like El Paso and San Diego. Aliens have burned to death while locked in car trunks; have had frozen fingers going north; and have been thrown overboard and drowned. Some have been subjected to forced labor to repay the cost of their trip. A chicken farmer in

Los Angeles was convicted of chaining Mexican illegals by the neck. In New York, Chinese illegals reported being forced to pay $500 in kickbacks to youth gangs who helped run a pipeline from Hong Kong which entered through Canada.

In 1979, of 18,500 smugglers apprehended, only 2,000 were convicted. They were probably not the ringleaders. Some were children and young teenagers who serve as guides or drivers for a $100 fee. If caught, they are often sentenced to probation and sent back across the border, where they pick up another load. Some, convicted of a felony, serve six months in jail. The average term is nineteen months; the maximum, five years. Some feel the penalties for smugglers are not stiff enough to deter repeated offenders.

BORDER PATROL

•The Border Patrol, created in 1924 as an agency of the Immigration and Naturalization Service, is charged with detecting and preventing illegal entry across the thousands of miles of land and water, barren deserts, shallow rivers, canyons, mountains, and oceans which form the borders of the United States.

• Members of the organization must be U.S. citizens under thirty-five years of age (or with previous experience in federal civilian law enforcement) and possess a driver's license. A written civil service examination, background investigation, and oral interview establish an applicant's eligibility. Excellent physical condition, including vision of 20/20 in each eye and binocular vision of 20/40 is required. Knowledge of Spanish gives additional credit.

•In 1981, this uniformed force numbered about 3,000 persons, 95 percent of them along the Mexican border in California, Arizona, New Mexico, and Texas. Yearly pay averaged $13,000. There was considerable disagreement as to the agency's effectiveness.

The Border Patrol claims its numbers are far too small to achieve meaningful control. The first four miles of a new $2 million electronic fence along the border was cut through in two dozen places as soon as it was built. Some holes were big enough for trucks to drive through. Smugglers keep a look-out on checkpoints and cross when they are closed because of bad weather or a shortage of agents. Agents say an additional force of 3,500 is needed. They also say their budget is too small to keep patrol cars in condition, or to pay informants like taxi drivers and hotel clerks. More advanced equipment, including rough-terrain vehicles and helicopters, is needed. Failure of the courts to fully prosecute offenders engaged in smuggling, especially juveniles, further hinders the Patrol's efforts to control it, some say. Agents have also claimed that fear of violating civil rights restricts their questioning of suspects.

Critics of the Patrol say that its members are often preju-diced, contemptuous, and racist. Mexicans resent their calling them "mojados" (wets), "wetbacks," and "tonks." Indian people crossing the Canadian border say they are forced to register as aliens although treaties grant them the right to enter freely. Members of the Patrol have been charged with shootings, beatings, rapes, torture, forced confessions, unlaw-ful arrests and deportations. A six-year-old Mexican girl rid-ing in a truck was shot during a chase by the Border Patrol. Patrolmen and agents have also been charged with issuing il-legal border crossing cards.

The Patrol replies that it often saves illegals' lives, rescuing them from death under difficult conditions. They say that il-legals are more often mistreated by "border bandits" who prey on them.

Experts do not agree on whether increasing the Border Pa-trol will solve the problem of illegals. "Give them a million men and they'd want a million-five," said one immigration official. California's Secretary of Health and Welfare, pro-posing an open border between the United States and Mexico, recommended that the Border Patrol be converted into a re-settlement agency for new immigrants.

With or without the Patrol, we will probably not solve the problem of illegal immigrants until we reduce the incentives for them to come.

ECONOMIC IMPACT

Do illegals contribute to the country's economic ills? Or are they sometimes made scapegoats for them? How do illegals affect the labor force? Labor claims that illegals take jobs from U.S. citizens and legal aliens. Civil rights groups fear that, since most illegals are young and unskilled, they take them particularly from young unskilled black workers. FAIR states that illegals force American workers to "compete with the unemployed of the world." Labor also claims that illegals are used in union-breaking operations. Some unions are beginning to try to organize them.

Because illegals fear discovery, prosecution, and deportation, they are often easy to exploit and slow to complain. They work, according to the Secretary of Labor, "both scared and hard," at the bottom of the labor market. They are, as a result, "creating a permanent underclass, outside the protection of our laws," with lower wages, poorer working conditions, and longer hours.

The Select Commission did not find that illegal immigrants lower wage levels or depress working conditions for the native population. (Some studies show that an increase in the number of unskilled workers produces an increase in the wages of skilled workers.) Nor is it clear that in the past they have taken their jobs. Illegals more often take jobs that native workers do not want, either because the pay is too low to attract them or because working conditions are not acceptable. They pick lettuce on farms in California and beans in Florida. They work as maids in motels. If the job pays a minimum wage of $3.10, or less than unemployment insurance, legal workers may not be interested. Recent evidence suggests, however, that illegals are beginning to seek better-paying jobs—in the construction industry, for instance.

It is not clear why unemployment among young blacks has continued to increase since 1954. Nor is it clear what causes unemployment in general. It is probably related more to the business cycle than to the presence of immigrants, legal or illegal. Population growth may affect wages more than the presence of illegals. When the "baby-boom" generation entered the labor market in the late sixties, earnings declined.

SOCIAL SERVICES
Do illegals burden the U.S. taxpayer? How much do illegals demand in social services? Is it more than they contribute to the economy? Illegals appear to make less use than citizens and legal aliens of taxpayer-financed social services, including health and welfare. Illegals are not usually anxious to go on record. When they use medical and hospital facilities, they pay their bills about as regularly as anyone else. (Although Los Angeles County sued the federal government in 1980 for $89 million in unpaid medical bills charged to illegals.) They pay taxes, including Social Security, at a higher rate relative to their earnings. Immigrants send money home if relatives still live in the country of origin. Illegals probably send more, as they more often leave family members behind. It is not clear how much of this money comes back to us in the purchase of American-produced goods.

Illegals probably increase the size of fire and police departments. What about our schools? The state of Texas estimated it spent $400 million a year in 1980 to educate the children of illegals who attended public schools. When the state tried to charge them tuition, an appeals judge declared it unconstitutional, and ruled that illegal immigrants have a right to free public education. Uneducated children probably pose a much more serious burden.

Whether they take jobs or burden our social services, however, the continued influx of illegal immigrants promotes disrespect for the law and seriously limits our ability to control our immigration policy.

SOLUTIONS
Nearly everyone agrees that we want to stop illegal immigration but few agree on how to do it. Most illegals come to the United States to get a job. If the opportunity to work were denied, illegal immigration would probably decline. Enforcement of existing labor laws, such as the wage and hour regula-

tions of the Fair Labor Standards Act, would help. If illegal labor were no longer cheap, it would probably be less attractive.

Employer sanctions are another possibility. If employers were faced with substantial fines for hiring illegals, they might be less apt to do so. Today, employers can be prosecuted for harboring or smuggling aliens but not for hiring them (the so-called Texas Proviso). It is ironic that it is illegal for undocumenteds to be here, but it is not illegal for employers to hire them. There is no federal law which prohibits it. A new law would be necessary. Eleven states and Puerto Rico have Fair Hiring laws and farm labor contractors are forbidden to recruit, hire, or employ illegals. So are defense contractors. The House of Representatives passed such legislation in 1972 and 1973 but the Senate took no action. President Carter requested its passage in 1977 with no success. A Fair Hiring amendment introduced in the Senate in 1980 prohibited the knowing employment of illegal immigrants by American employers. It died in session.

If a Fair Hiring law is passed, it must be enforced. Voluntary compliance alone might not work. Civil and criminal penalties might be necessary. And there must be a way to identify workers who are eligible to work. One way to do that is with a national work permit or work authorization card for all workers, citizens and aliens alike: a highly controversial proposal.

WORK AUTHORIZATION CARD

A work authorization card would have to be foolproof and counterfeit-resistant. It would probably include a photograph or perhaps a fingerprint or signature (but not the home address) of the worker. It could be issued to workers when they enter the labor force or change jobs within it. The Social Security card, which since 1972 has required proof of identity, might be used. It is now used for taxpayer identification and, as automation and computerization increases, by banks, hospitals, colleges, and government agencies.

A number of European countries, including France, West Germany, Belgium, Italy, Luxembourg, Switzerland, and Rumania, have some form of worker identification. So does South Africa. Some highly industrialized countries, Britain, Canada, and Japan, for example, do not.

Studies in the United States show opposition to a national identification system. The main fear is that it might lead to an invasion of privacy and violation of civil liberties and increasing government control over individuals. Some see in the system the threat of a police state and envision George Orwell's *1984* becoming a reality. Some object to the card as an "internal passport." Others fear law enforcement agencies might improperly use the system in investigations such as seeking fugitives, for instance. The American Civil Liberties Union has been active in opposition to the cards.

Hispanic-Americans fear the cards would lead to harassment of workers with foreign looks or accents. Employers, penalized for hiring illegals, might discriminate more against Hispanics and other minorities suspected of being illegals. (Others say the card would protect minorities from discrimination.) The cards themselves might lead to increased fraud.

Opponents of a work authorization system suggest the government try harder to enforce existing laws governing immigration, wage and hour regulations, and tax laws. They also cite the expense of putting the system into effect. Employers say it is the government's job to crack down on illegal immigration, not theirs.

Supporters of the cards see it as the only way we can hope to enforce the laws and a lesser evil than the prospect of increasing numbers of illegals. Among them are the AFL-CIO, FAIR, and Theodore M. Hesburgh, president of Notre Dame and chairman of the government's Select Commission. Hesburgh believes the work place, not the border, is the place to stop illegals. He emphasizes that the card would be required to be shown only once: at the time of hiring. Hesburgh says: "We cannot require employers to not hire illegals if we don't have some means of identifying who is legal and who is not . . . Give me a better solution and I'd be for it."

A constitutional amendment has been proposed to protect civil liberties and the rights of privacy in the advent of a work authorization system. A central labor force data bank has been suggested as an alternative.

An editorial in *The New York Times,* supporting the card, stated: "It is no more sensible to reject the identification idea because of potential problems than to ban telephones because they can be tapped." In its final report, the Select Commission skirted the issue and voted eight to seven for "some more secure method of identification" and proposed continued use of birth certificates, driver's licenses, and immigration cards as well.

OTHER SOLUTIONS

We might increase the Mexican quota and allow more Mexicans to enter legally. Mexico has always questioned the Mexican–U.S. boundary set by the Treaty of Guadalupe-Hidalgo in 1848. Many Mexicans feel they have been established in the Southwest long enough to have the right to be there in numbers now. Does a "Good Neighbor" close its borders to neighbors who want to enter? Should Mexicans be held to an annual quota of 20,000 when many more wish to come? "It is not a crime to look for work," says the President of Mexico, "and I refuse to consider it as such."

Another proposal is a temporary worker program which would allow aliens to enter for a specified period to work in jobs Americans don't want. Programs which exist in Europe today usually require workers to move out after a number of months so they don't become settled. They are not allowed to become citizens.

Wyoming sheep ranchers say they cannot attract domestic workers. Farmers in Virginia say they cannot find Americans to harvest seasonal crops. Why can't they hire willing workers from Mexico? The economies of many border states depend on the cheap labor of illegals, not only itinerant farm labor, but employees of hotels and restaurants, garment industries, assembly lines, construction industries, and hospitals. In southern Texas, they are part of everyday life.

From 1942 to 1964, we had our "bracero" program with Mexico. After World War II, more than 10 million "guest workers" migrated from southern Europe and the Mediterranean region to northern Europe to supply labor for its post-war economic development. Many of these programs have now been stopped. It was found that many of the "guests" outstayed their welcome.

Opponents of a temporary worker program including organized labor and Hispanic Americans say it encourages illegals and "creates a class of exploited persons who pose a threat to domestic workers." They say employers should increase wages and improve working conditions and pass on the pay increases in higher prices for lettuce and motel rooms. Otherwise, we are in effect subsidizing these industries.

AMNESTY

There is a widespread belief, supported by the Select Commission, that we should legalize the undocumenteds who are now in the United States with some sort of *amnesty*. Except for the Mexicans who flow back and forth across the border in response to the job market, many illegals have been here for years. They have acquired homes, raised children, paid taxes and become assimilated into our society. There would be no way to pry them loose without massive raids and deportations. So-called area control operations in which INS officers "sweep" a wide area seeking suspected illegals, often without evidence, cause accusations of racial discrimination and are one of the major complaints against the service. Mass expulsions would be neither practical nor humane.

The Democratic administration proposed amnesty in 1977 for loyal undocumented workers who had been here for seven years without causing problems, were learning English, attending school, working and paying taxes. No action was taken in Congress.

If amnesty were granted, what would be the effect on state and local health and education facilities as illegals surface? Would legalizing their status as immigrants with the right to work and become citizens attract even more illegals?

Opponents of amnesty say granting mass pardons to those who violate our laws weakens our laws and encourages further violations.

A final suggestion in the effort to control the influx of illegals is that we support major efforts toward economic development in Mexico to equalize the forces which "push" people from Latin America and "pull" them to the United States. We cannot hope to solve all of Mexico's problems of overpopulation and poverty. But, should we continue to allow large-scale immigration in hopes it will serve as a stopgap to social and political upheaval there?

Whatever we do, we should have a policy that tells us how many can come, how they should enter, and how they should be employed when they're here. And we should stick to that policy.

ILLEGALS AND THE CENSUS

In 1980, the United States took its twentieth ten-year census. Our first census, in 1790, counted "the whole Number of free persons . . . and excluding Indians not taxed, three fifths of all other persons." The Fourteenth Amendment in 1868 dropped the qualifications and blacks and, later, Indians, were fully counted.

Representation in Congress and many forms of federal aid are determined by population. Illegals can make a difference. Should they be counted?

The 1980 Census included in its count 20 million aliens. The Census does not question their status as either legal or illegal. As many as 5 million might be illegal. Some say 6 to 8 million. An attempt by the House of Representatives to discount use of the figures in determining how many representatives the states were entitled to was voted down.

The Federation for American Immigration Reform opposed counting illegals and sued the Census Bureau, saying its figures should not be used in reapportionment for it gave illegals legal status and political representation in Congress they did not deserve. Visitors here legally as tourists are not counted. If they become "overstayers," they might be. FAIR said counting illegals could take representatives from thirteen states and add to those of six others, denying and distorting proper representation. FAIR wanted a separate count of illegals. FAIR lost its suit, but appealed to the Supreme Court.

The Border Patrol claimed that efforts to include illegals in the census count hampered their efforts. Immigration officials asked for a moratorium on crackdowns on illegals while the census took place, restricting raids in order to get cooperation of Hispanic Americans. (Meanwhile, restriction protected the INS from accusations of brutality and false arrest and violations of the Fourth Amendment ban on unreasonable searches and seizures.) A Labor Department aide accused the Service of abrogating its enforcement responsibilities in a political response to pressure by Hispanics. Some blacks fear they will lose representation, hard come by, in areas with larger concentrations of Hispanics.

Foreigners have always been included in past censuses. Today, some people are concerned about the suspected heavy concentration of illegals in California, New York, and Chicago. New York City, with 600,000 registered aliens, may have as many as 700,000 illegals. Two congressional seats and millions of dollars in city revenues are at stake.

On the other hand, some feel the Census misses many people in inner-city neighborhoods where aliens, minorities, and the poor are most apt to reside. New York City disputed the results of the 1980 Census for that reason and set up its own program to locate the uncounted.

The Census Bureau says that illegals are here, must be provided with services such as fire and police, deserve representation and aid, and must be counted. Hispanics say illegals pay taxes but don't collect refunds or apply for Social Security and unemployment insurance so they deserve to be counted and receive other benefits.

The chances are the Census missed many illegals anyhow. They're not apt to want to be counted.

*For the diverse, alien peoples
flocking to this country, the
trade unions in their imperfect way
served as a primary vehicle for
working-class unity and for entry
into the American environment.*
> David Brody
> *Howard Encyclopedia
> of Ethnic Groups*

IMMIGRATION AND ORGANIZED LABOR

The foreign-born have always formed a significant part of our work force. The Immigration Service was a bureau of the Department of Labor from 1903 to 1940. Before World War I, immigrants accounted for about 14 percent of the country's population but they accounted for 25 percent of the workers in transportation; 36 percent in manufacturing; and 45 percent in mining. Among blue-collar workers, they accounted for nearly 60 percent of the labor force. In Boston in 1850, 80 percent of the laborers were Irish; in Milwaukee in 1860, 58 percent were German; in 1907, Slavs formed 80 percent of the work force at Pittsburgh's Carnegie Steel.

The "old" immigration played an important role in organizing the labor movement. Samuel Gompers (1850–1924), the first president of the American Federation of Labor, was an English immigrant. The first unions in the United States were organized on craft lines and composed mostly of English-speaking skilled workers and artisans. The "new" immigrants, largely unskilled, were not readily assimilated into their ranks.

The labor movement was an important factor in closing the door on America's traditional open-door immigration policy. The AFL claimed credit for the Chinese Exclusion Act and supported the requirement of a literacy test which, according to Gompers, "would exclude hardly any natives of Great Britain, Ireland, Germany, France, or Scandinavia. It will shut out a considerable number of southern Italians and of Slavs and other[s] equally or more undesirable and injurious."

Early in the twentieth century, the radical IWW (Industrial Workers of the World) attempted to organize foreigners, including Asians, "no matter what [their] religion, fatherland, or trade." But the presence of socialists and communists among immigrants from eastern Europe (especially Russians, Finns, and Jews) worked against them.

The AFL joined the restrictionists and came down on the side of "racial purity and strength" to endorse the quota system in 1921. Its opposition to unrestricted immigration was based on fear of an overcrowded labor market and immigrants' willingness to work for low wages under poor conditions, which undermined labor standards. Some of the opposition, however, including the opposition to blacks who moved in increasing numbers from farms of the South to industrial cities of the North, was clearly racist.

The rise of the CIO (Congress of Industrial Organizations) in 1938 and the development of industry-wide unions which organized all workers "regardless of skill, race, nationality, religion or politics," helped to bring immigrants into the labor movement and into the American environment. CIO organizers tried to speak to them in their own languages, used their foreign-language press, and worked with fraternal and social organizations in Polish, Lithuanian, Russian, Serbian, and Croatian communities.

The union of the AFL and CIO in 1955 pledged "to encourage all workers without regard to race, creed, color, national origin or ancestry to share equally in the full benefits of union organization."

Mexicans, Puerto Ricans, Chinese, and blacks continue to be exploited in low-wage industries where labor organization is at a minimum. A few unions, such as that of the Chicano farm workers under Cesar Chavez, gain power through ethnic identity. Anti-black sentiment in the South may hold back union organization there.

Organized labor continues to oppose large-scale immigration in the belief that immigrant labor takes jobs from citizens and resident aliens and lowers wages and working standards. The Secretary of Labor stated in 1980 that control of illegal immigration could cut unemployment to 4 percent. Resident workers feel that refugees and family members entering the United States are not carefully screened for their effects on the labor market. They feel that labor certification, to protect American workers by defining areas where American workers are not available, is not effective. The unions oppose any form of temporary foreign worker program as a form of exploitation.

Newsweek reported in 1980 that "the only sight more horrifying than an immigrant on welfare was one with a job." However, immigration—except for the unknown impact of illegals—generally accounts for only a small percentage of labor market growth. Studies seem to show that immigration has helped to raise the standards of English-speaking workers, and especially of skilled workers. In times of economic depression, foreign workers are usually the first to be released.

Some unions are beginning to organize alien workers, including illegal aliens, and there is evidence that they are taking a new look at immigrants, especially refugees, as an economic fact of life. With the influx of Cubans and Haitians into Miami, an AFL-CIO spokesman said that competition for jobs from refugees should not be an argument for keeping them out. Instead, more jobs should be created if they are needed.

"The worst thing that could happen to trade unionism is for groups of workers to be set against each other in a competition for scarce jobs," said the federation's president. "The role of this country as a place of refuge for victims of oppression is a matter of the highest priority."

Republicans are proud that our people have opened their arms and hearts to strangers from abroad, and we favor an immigration policy which is consistent with this tradition.

Republican Party Platform, 1980

America's roots are founded in the immigrants and refugees who have come to our shores to build new lives in a new world. The Democratic Party pledges to honor our historical commitment to this heritage.

Democratic Party Platform, 1980

IMMIGRATION AND POLITICS

Immigrants have always played an important role in American politics. Ethnic traditions and religious beliefs have always been factors in determining party loyalties, reflecting party stands on such issues as abolition of slavery, Prohibition, women's suffrage, morality, religion, and, of course, immigration.

In general, immigrants from northern Europe, English-speakers, and Protestants have traditionally supported the Republican party. Those from southern and eastern Europe, Catholics, Jews, and blacks have favored the Democrats. There are many exceptions, of course, but within these broad outlines, basic group loyalties do exist.

Economic conditions and, occasionally, the appeal of a particular candidate, can cause alliances to shift. The Great Depression won many Republican votes for Democrat Franklin Roosevelt in 1936. Teddy Roosevelt, a Republican, attracted Polish voters, normally Democratic, in 1904. And in 1952,

Eisenhower, also a Republican, appealed to many Democrats as a war hero and an anti-Communist.

Some national groups have been more active in politics than others. The Irish particularly, who lacked opportunity in many other fields, gravitated to politics. The Democratic machines of many eastern cities were built and maintained by them.

Today, the Irish, many of them middle class, educated, and affluent, tend less to form a solidly Democratic group. Some famous Irish politicians are Alfred E. Smith (Governor of New York); Senator Joseph McCarthy; Senator Eugene McCarthy; and John, Robert, and Edward Kennedy.

Poles, Czechs, Lithuanians, and Greeks generally vote Democratic too, although they have never been a major force on a national scale. Senator Edmund Muskie of Maine was the first Polish politician to gain national prominence. Scandinavians tend toward the Republicans; northern Italians (part of the "old" immigration) are mostly Republican (the party of former Governor John Volpe of Massachusetts); southern Italians, mostly Democratic.

The largest ethnic group, the Germans, have tended to split their political loyalties. In the past, their opposition to Prohibition, Nativism, and strict Sunday observance, their support of bilingualism in schools, and their antiwar sentiment led them to the Democrats. The depression of 1896 shifted them to the Republicans.

There have been many socialists and reformers among the Germans. As a result of World Wars I and II, when they experienced bitter American hostility, the Germans have tended to downplay their ethnicity and are no longer considered an important political bloc.

German Jews were Republican until the depression of the 1930s. Eastern European Jews were mostly Democrats but supported Theodore Roosevelt and Taft. Franklin Roosevelt's liberal policies and strong opposition to the Nazis, coupled with Harry Truman's pro-Israel stance, attracted both groups to the Democratic fold. Herbert Lehman was a famous governor of New York; Jacob Javits, a well-known senator.

An 1889 cartoon—perhaps the original "melting pot."

Hispanics are fast becoming a major force in American politics, tending toward the Democrats for economic and religious reasons. The Hispanic vote is not homogeneous, however. Puerto Ricans, Mexicans, Dominicans, and Cubans all have different sets of problems. Only the Cubans came as political exiles; the others, largely for economic relief. Hispanic illegals try to keep a low profile and don't often participate in politics.

The first wave of Cubans, who hoped ultimately to return to influence in Cuba, were largely political conservatives who opposed any attempt at conciliation with the Castro government. The latest wave will probably be different. Brought up under Communism, they may join with more liberal Mexicans, Puerto Ricans, and Dominicans to form a significant political bloc.

Second-generation Cubans applauded the Democrats' efforts at reconciliation with Cuba, the easing of travel restrictions, and the release of political prisoners which accompanied the Freedom Flotilla (which a Democratic administration generously welcomed).

In general, the end of mass immigration lessened the importance of ethnic considerations as a political force, but politicians are still marching in Columbus Day parades, eating kielbasa in honor of Casimir Pulaski, and donning the guayabera shirt and sombrero to woo the ethnic voter.

The first order of business is
to get somebody in there that
can turn that place around.
   Congressional aide quoted
   in *The New York Times,*
   December 28, 1980

THE INS

Everybody talks about the INS, but nobody does much about it. The Immigration and Naturalization Service is accused, at best, of being ineffective, poorly managed and administered. At worst, it is accused of large-scale corruption and "institutionalized racism," of lacking "competence, professionalism, and human kindness." Agents are accused of taking bribes and kickbacks; complaints of bias against Filipinos, Chinese, Central and South Americans are common. Without strong and established leadership, morale is low.

"That place is a disaster area over there," summed up one U.S. Senator.

The INS regulates the admission of all foreigners into the United States. In 1978, U.S. borders were crossed 277 million times. Nearly 10 million aliens were admitted; 600,000 of them were immigrants. In addition, 5 million aliens reported to the INS under its annual "alien address" requirement. The INS determines which aliens shall be admitted and the conditions of their stay; which shall be excluded; and which shall be deported. It is also responsible for the naturalization process.

In 1979 and 1980, the INS had the job of tracing 60,000 Iranian students in the United States; processing 125,000 Cuban and 11,000 Haitian refugees who arrived unannounced on our southern doorstep; trying, with depleted forces, to guard the Mexican border against illegal crossings; and deciding whether a twelve-year-old Russian boy should be granted asylum after refusing to accompany his parents back to the USSR.

The INS inspects the papers of all arrivals at ports of entry. (Animals need import permits too, certifying that they are disease-free.) It issues the "green cards," so highly valued by immigrants, which give them the right to work in the United States. It also issues pink cards to nonimmigrant Canadians crossing the border; blue or salmon-beige cards to Mexicans. Alien crewmen receive landing permits for a period not to exceed twenty-nine days, but jumping ship is a popular form of "overstaying." The INS is supposed to see that temporary visitors leave on time.

Defenders of the Service say they are far behind on sorting and filing immigration records because their equipment is hopelessly outdated. Between 1979 and 1981, they were without a permanent director for over a year. Because of lack of support from Congress and the President, they lack funds to hire adequate staff, to buy automated equipment, and to efficiently enforce the law. Besides, the law is complicated and ambiguous, making immigrants easy prey for unethical lawyers, consultants, travel agents, and others posing as immigration officials. Two United States Congressmen were convicted in 1980 of taking bribes to introduce special legislation allowing fictitious Arab sheiks to immigrate, resulting in the first expulsion from Congress since the Civil War.

With fewer than fifty immigration judges, there are many delays in deportations and appeals. Deportation rulings can be appealed to the Board of Immigration Appeals, the U.S. Court of Appeals, and the Supreme Court.

Future policy will probably try to simplify the grounds for exclusion and perhaps incorporate a statute of limitations on violations of INS law as grounds for deportation. In the roundup of Iranians following the taking of American hostages in Iran in 1979, a student was charged with shoplifting a grape and threatened with deportation for committing a crime of "moral turpitude." A West Virginia judge acquitted him. However, an alien who overstayed his visa by nine years was deported because he stole olives for food and wood for fire during World War II in Italy. His father and brothers were naturalized citizens, but he was refused an immigrant visa because of crimes he committed at age nineteen.

Some feel that the functions of enforcement and service should be separated, with the enforcement responsibility going back to the Treasury Department where it began. Then, some believe, the INS could concentrate on service. In that role, INS agents might no longer be tainted with a discriminatory attitude toward the aliens they are meant to be helping.

*Everywhere immigrants have
enriched and strengthened
the fabric of American life.*
                    John F. Kennedy

*Today a wide-open door is an
invitation to national disaster.*
                    FAIR

BURDEN OR BENEFIT?

Immigration experts are fond of saying that "Twentieth-Century America has grown up in the shadow of the Statue of Liberty." They mean that we perceive ourselves as welcoming in ever-increasing numbers the "huddled masses" of the world, sometimes without concern for their impact on the quality of our own lives. Polls on immigration taken over the last decade show, however, that most Americans want to reduce current immigration levels.

Immigrants made a decisive contribution to our nation during its growing years. Do they still benefit us? Or have they become a burden we cannot afford to bear?

Environmentalists say we cannot support increasing numbers of people who strain our natural resources. We have already experienced water shortages, power failures, and fuel crises. In addition, forest products, textiles, and basic minerals are in short supply.

With increased urbanization, our agricultural land declines, creating food shortages. If these shortages grow more severe, we will no longer be able to export food to needy nations.

Are we "drawing from a vast pool of poverty beyond our borders" ask the new restrictionists, envisioning endless applicants for immigration from Third World countries.

Immigration, they say, instead of relieving Third World population pressures, actually hurts underdeveloped countries by taking their most capable people. They are young, productive, hardworking, and motivated to achieve, sometimes the only highly trained and skilled citizens. (The Federation for American Immigration Reform proposes that the Irish would be better off today if they had stayed home after the potato famine, received international aid, and set about controlling their population.)

Some believe that disadvantaged nations should be encouraged to deal with population pressures at home rather than trying to solve their problems by exporting their people.

Although racism has largely disappeared as a factor in our immigration policy, some restrictionists point with alarm to the numbers of Spanish-speaking immigrants who are entering. They fear increasing racial and ethnic tension and say an "imbalance" of ethnic diversity is being created. Some ethnic differences among immigrants have been found: non-Hispanic whites, Japanese, and second-generation Chinese appear to fare better than Filipinos and Mexicans, perhaps reflecting the level of discrimination they experience.

Today's immigrants come largely from countries with higher rates of fertility than our own. They may increase our population more than the natural increase.

For those whose goal is Zero Population Growth, where the number of births is offset by the number of deaths, immigration is seen to offset any decline in the birth rate which we achieve. The Select Commission, on the other hand, concluded that, if our present fertility rate of 1.8 percent were to remain constant, annual immigration of 850,000 would result in population stabilization by the year 2003. Furthermore, as immigrants climb the economic ladder, they tend to conform to our standards.

"The myths of the bountiful frontier, with its limitless resources and ever-fruitful land" are gone, says FAIR. Of the major immigrant-receiving countries in the world today, only the United States shuns significant restriction. Our standard of living is at stake: jobs, per capita income, advanced social conditions are all threatened.

Have we reached the cut-off point? Immigration had many positive effects in the past. Industry expanded as new workers entered the labor force, helping native workers improve their own position. Costs of production fell, and as a result, prices did too. Markets expanded as consumption grew, and, as Oscar Handlin noted, "each new group pushed upward the level of its predecessors."

There were negative effects, of course. Towns grew into cities, tenements and slums developed, causing the problems of poverty and the need for relief.

Where do we stand today? The open spaces are closed. Our population has grown to over 225 million. Eight percent of our labor force often faces unemployment. The rate of economic growth has declined. In a changed United States, can we still afford to welcome immigrants?

A federal study in 1980 showed that immigrants, from the time they set foot on our shores, contribute more in taxes than they take out in public services.

Immigrant families begin to earn as much as native families within two to six years of their arrival; in ten years, they have passed them. Children of immigrants, after they have overcome the language barrier and culture shock, generally complete more years of school and college than our own native-born. Professor Julian L. Simon, who conducted a study at the University of Illinois, concluded that "the average immigrant is a remarkably good investment for taxpayers."

Refugees take a little longer to achieve their goals, possibly because their decision to migrate was a choice determined by political forces. Many would rather return to their homelands and are not as strongly motivated to work.

Immigrants may be selectively superior to begin with, a Yale professor has suggested. Immigrants have made significant contributions to the cultural, social, political, and economic life of our country. Economically, they improve our standard of living by starting their own businesses and creating jobs and by exporting our goods to their homelands. They contribute more in taxes than they use in services. They do not markedly increase welfare or other social service costs, except for some initial health services and remedial and bilingual education programs.

In spite of many claims to the contrary, the Select Commission found that immigrants do not displace native workers to a significant degree, although their impact on the most disadvantaged segment of the working population may be significant. Whether decreasing immigration would solve that problem is uncertain.

Immigrants represent human resources that continue to enrich our culture and add to our national diversity. Our future immigration policy must surely reflect the realities of our growing population, dwindling resources, expanding labor force, and threatened environment. But closing the door on future immigration may cause us to lose more than we gain.

*The law is the last result
of human wisdom acting
upon human experience for
the benefit of the public.*
                    Samuel Johnson

FUTURE POLICY

The Golden Door to immigration is no longer wide open but
it is still ajar. Immigrants have been a great strength to the
American nation. Nobody wants to close the door tight. Immigration in 1981 was expected to reach about 700,000. Most
people thought they could live with that. The government's
Select Commission concluded that we could accept 850,000
immigrants a year without undue population growth, and
recommended a numerical ceiling of 350,000.

More people will continue to want to come to the United
States than we will be able to accept. We must determine what
proportion of the newcomers will be relatives of U.S. citizens
and resident aliens; how many will be refugees; and how many
will be so-called seed immigrants, without previous ties.

Most important, our new policy should have a flexibility
which our current policy lacks. National quotas might be
dropped. In a year when large numbers of refugees enter, the
number of family members and "seed" immigrants might de-
crease, and vice versa. Family reunification preference might

apply only to "nuclear family" members: husbands, wives, and minor children of U.S. citizens (who are now exempt from ceilings).

Ceilings should be subject to review at established intervals, and factors such as economic productivity, population growth, and the rate of unemployment might be considered in this review.

Coming to grips with illegals is essential in achieving a viable immigration policy. Effective enforcement probably requires some form of employer sanctions and work authorization card and might be preceded by a one-time amnesty, perhaps related to the number of years the illegals have lived in this country. We must also clear the decks of the backlog of visa applicants, including relatives of newly legalized aliens, perhaps feeding in 100,000 a year over a five-year period.

Our guiding principles will continue to be family reunification, the plight of refugees, and the needs of the economy. In the future, we will probably also consider our depleted resources, our environment, the level of social and racial justice in our own society. We must assure that the disadvantaged of our own nation share in the benefits of our society as we extend them to people of other nations.

Finally, we must pursue foreign policies which encourage development in underdeveloped countries, creating jobs and improving their standards of living. Poverty, hunger, and oppressive governments around the world still drive the needy of all nations to our shores. We cannot turn our backs on them.

FOR FURTHER READING

BOOKS

Brownstone, David M., *et al. Island of Hope, Island of Tears.* New York: Rawson, Wade Publishers, 1979.

Coppa, Frank J., and Curran, Thomas J. *The Immigrant Experience in America.* Boston: Twayne Publishers, 1977.

Fermi, Laura. *Illustrious Immigrants.* Chicago: University of Chicago Press, 1972.

Handlin, Oscar. *A Pictorial History of Immigration.* New York: Crown, 1972.

———. *The Uprooted,* 2nd ed. Boston: Atlantic Monthly Press, 1973.

Hansen, Marcus Lee. *The Immigrant in American History.* New York: Harper and Row, 1971.

Hoff, Rhoda. *America's Immigrants.* New York: Henry Z. Walck, 1967.

Kennedy, John F. *A Nation of Immigrants.* New York: Harper and Row, 1964.

Neidle, Cecyle S. *Great Immigrants.* Boston: Twayne Publishers, 1972.

Taylor, Philip. *The Distant Magnet.* New York: Harper and Row, 1971.

Thernstrom, Stephan, *et al.,* eds. *Harvard Encyclopedia of American Ethnic Groups.* Cambridge, Mass.: Harvard University Press, 1980.

Tripp, Eleanor B. *To America.* New York: Harcourt Brace Jovanovich, 1969.

Tyler, Poyntz. *Immigration and the United States.* New York: H. W. Wilson, 1956.

Weisberger, Bernard A. *The American People.* New York: American Heritage, 1971.

Wheeler, Thomas, ed. *The Immigrant Experience*. New York: Penguin Books, 1972.

Ziegler, Benjamin Munn. *Immigration: An American Dilemma*. Lexington, Mass.: D. C. Heath, 1953.

GOVERNMENT PUBLICATIONS

U.S. Department of Justice. *Our Immigration: A Brief Account of Immigration to the United States,* rev., prepared by the Immigration and Naturalization Service (Washington, D.C.: Government Printing Office, 1977).

U.S. Select Commission on Immigration and Refugee Policy.

Semi-Annual Report to Congress. March 1, 1980.

Semi-Annual Report to Congress. September 1, 1980.

Newsletters, November 1979–December 1980.

Background Papers:

Immigrants: How Many?

From Where?

Illegal Migrants: What do we do about those who are already here?

Illegal Migration: Inhibiting Future Flows.

The Economic Impacts of Illegal Migrants.

ARTICLES

Adler, Jerry, *et al.* "The New Immigrants." *Newsweek,* July 7, 1980, pp. 26–31.

Graham, Otis L., Jr. "Illegal Immigration and the New Reform Movement." Immigration Paper II. Federation for American Immigration Reform, February 1980.

————. "Illegal Immigration and the New Restrictionism." *Center Magazine,* May–June 1979, pp. 54–64.

Szulc, Tad. "The Refugee Explosion." *New York Times Magazine,* November 23, 1980, pp. 136–141.

Tanton, John. "Rethinking Immigration Policy." Immigration Paper I. Federation for American Immigration Reform, January 1980.

Teitelbaum, Michael S. "Right Versus Right: Immigration and Refugee Policy in the United States." *Foreign Affairs,* Fall 1980, pp. 21–59.

Young, Harry F. "Refugees—An International Obligation." U.S. Department of State *Bulletin,* December 1979, pp. 11–19.

INDEX